Sizzling
Customer Service

Success Tips from Top Trainers, Speakers and Consultants
to Turn Your Career and Business Red Hot!

Linda,
Wishing you more success
with less stress!

Sam

Compiled by **Doug Smart**

James &
Brookfield

J&B

Publishers

Sizzling Customer Service

Cover Design:	PAULA CHANCE
Editing:	GELIA DOLCIMASCOLO
Proof Reader:	LAURA JOHNSON
Book Layout:	DARLENE NICHOLAS

For more information, contact:
James & Brookfield Publishers
P.O. Box 768024
Roswell, GA 30076
(770) 587-9784

Library of Congress Catalog Number 98-67156

ISBN: 0-9658893-4-3

10 9 8 7 6 5 4 3 2 1

Dedication

Dedicated to our Moms and Dads for teaching us the importance of thoughtful manners. Back then, "practicing manners" was a nuisance. Now, we understand their true significance in a world starved for quality customer service.

Table of Contents

Foreword

You are only as good as the last contact between your best customer and your worst front line employee.

Never mind how hard you have worked in the past to develop a reputation for excellence in customer relations. No matter the expense you have incurred or the other resources you have expended to make your customers feel valued and appreciated. They will remember their last experience with your front line employees.

For many years I have been a fan of Delta Air Lines. "Delta is ready when you are," "We love to fly and it shows," and "You will love the way we fly" were more than just advertising slogans as far as I was concerned. I loved Delta Air Lines. Their distinctive red, white, and blue triangle logo really did give me a warm and fuzzy feeling. On the rare occasions when I had no choice but to fly another airline, I literally felt like I was coming back home when I connected to a Delta flight.

In my role as a seminar leader I frequently used stories about my positive experiences with Delta Air Lines to illustrate the "Three C's" of customer service and satisfaction:

- Care
- Competence
- Communication

Delta showed me how much they truly cared for my business when my commuter flight from Long Island to Boston was delayed due to excessive air traffic. We finally landed in Boston about five minutes after my flight home to Atlanta was scheduled to take off. As we touched down, I looked out the window and saw a speeding white station wagon with the familiar Delta logo on its door pull abreast of our airplane. It followed alongside as we slowed, pulled off the runway onto a taxiway, and eased to a stop.

The flight attendant asked me to come forward as she opened the door of the aircraft. While I descended the stairs, the station wagon driver removed my luggage from the hold and placed it into the vehicle. A gracious Delta representative with a walkie-talkie in her hand greeted me courteously and they whisked me across the taxiways to the big Delta jet being held at the gate waiting to take me to Atlanta.

Delta showed their competence and outstanding customer communications on more occasions than I can remember. A last minute canceled flight to Hawaii didn't even slow down the hard-earned vacation my wife, Barbara, and I were looking forward to. Delta had us on another airplane within fifteen minutes and arranged for our luggage, which had been checked and was already aboard the original aircraft, to be transported to our destination by another airline. A Delta representative wearing a trademark red coat was waiting just for us as we de-planed in Los Angeles. He informed us that our uninterrupted continuation to Hawaii was assured and let us know that our luggage was OK. As we walked off the plane in Honolulu, our names were being called with instructions to claim our luggage.

Sooner or later every service provider has problems, and companies known for customer service excellence, like Delta Air Lines used to be, understand this and have efficient recovery systems in place to deal with those problems when they occur. About 10 minutes after departure on a flight from San Francisco to Atlanta, the pilot announced that the slats along the leading edge of the wing, which provide added lift during takeoff, would not retract and that we had to return to San Francisco. There were the usual groans among the passengers, but Delta had tables set up in the concourse. They were arranged according to last name and staffed by a platoon of red-coated specialists prepared to do whatever was required to get their passengers rerouted and on the way. Delta had everyone rescheduled and I, along with most of the other passengers, was aboard a replacement flight to Atlanta in just over an hour. Delta kept us informed about connecting flights and other needed information continuously on that flight and I saw only one person complaining as we de-planed in Atlanta. Again, Delta had provided good service, and they delivered it well.

Not long after that, I was riding in a van from the St. Louis airport to my hotel. A Delta flight crew just happened to be on the van, also, along with a flight crew from another major airline. The van made an intermediate stop and the Delta crew got off. After the van doors closed, one of the flight attendants from the other airline said, "God, I hate those people! And I hate their damn red coats! They are so sweet and everybody just loves them. Nobody can be that good."

But they were. Delta was special and their customers were the most loyal in the world. I loved to tell my audiences about Delta Air Lines. No doubt about it, Delta was my airline.

And, my how things change!

As I write this, I am sitting in the Akron-Canton airport on a hot summer afternoon. I have just conducted a sales negotiation conference at Kent State University and driven to the airport and turned my rental car in. When I checked in at the Delta connection counter about 4:40, I expected to kill some time waiting for my 6:42 flight to Cincinnati. When I checked the departure monitor, I saw that there was a five o'clock flight to Cincinnati and hurried to try to get on board as a standby.

I arrived at the gate at precisely 4:48 by the clock on the wall and saw the five o'clock plane to Cincinnati taxiing away in the distance. I couldn't believe it! My watch showed 4:51. Any way you figure it, the plane had clearly left the gate about ten minutes early.

If I was disbelieving, the young man in front of me was absolutely dumbfounded — and he was furious. He was trying to explain to the gate agent that he was going to miss his connection in Cincinnati and that his wife and two-year-old child had already left home driving three hours to pick him up and that he couldn't reach her. He said that he had been on time for his flight, that he spent $60,000 a year with Delta Air Lines, and that he couldn't understand why the plane on which he had a confirmed reservation had left early — with a number of empty seats, no less. I don't remember ever seeing anyone more frustrated.

The gate agent (we'll call her Elaine) didn't care, and then she made things worse. Elaine was a pain. She was loud, unfeeling, and in-his-face rude. As he turned away, I spoke to him and we began bemoaning the unbelievable decline in Delta's service and attitude toward their customers. As we walked away, Elaine just couldn't leave it alone. She very abrasively butted into our conversation and told us that Delta's surveys showed their customers' number one concerns was on-time departures. She proceeded to lecture us and informed us that if we were going to fly Delta in the future we had better be on board ten minutes before scheduled departure or we could plan on getting left behind.

Elaine, we don't give a damn about meaningless on-time departures. Not too long ago I was sitting in a window seat on an airplane in Chicago, which belongs to one of your competitors. When the time for departure arrived, they closed the aircraft door and pulled the ramp back a few feet.

Statistically they had another on-time departure to enter into the records even though we continued to sit at the gate.

A minute or so later a disheveled, out-of-breath young woman carrying a baby on one arm and towing a toddler with the other rushed to the end of the ramp and stood staring in disbelief. She pleaded with the attendant to let her board the aircraft, then burst into tears. I couldn't hear what was being said, but the body language was unmistakable. The visual image remains burned into my memory, and it was heart wrenching. She was led away still pleading and crying. We finally pulled away from the gate nearly fifteen minutes later.

Elaine, we don't care about your statistics. Given the volume of air traffic these days and legitimate concerns for safety, arrival time is far less dependent on departure time than you would have us believe. Your departure times are much more about self-serving statistics than they are about selflessly serving your customers.

What we do care about is not being made to feel like cattle, being treated well, and arriving as close to on time as air-safety conditions permit. We also care about not having to put up with the likes of you.

Although I know that customers don't complain because they don't know who to complain to, don't figure it's worth the effort, and don't believe it will do any good, I did find the manger on duty and complained about the way my fellow traveler and I had been treated. I gave her my business card and frequent flyer number and asked her to make it official. She shook my hand and told me what a good service provider Elaine was. She lied.

A few years ago I would have received a letter from Delta, and possibly a phone call, but that's the last I have heard of this incident. I probably had the wrong person, anyway, and I'm very sure it didn't do any good. It might have been worth the effort if it had made me feel better, but it really didn't. Somehow, it just made me feel sadder.

I was at the gate for my 6:42 flight to Cincinnati twenty minutes early to be sure I didn't get left behind. The young man who spends $60,000.00 a year with Delta was there, too. He had not been able to reach his wife. We started boarding the plane just before 7:00 and took off around 7:20, not quite forty minutes late. Elaine had gone home and the new gate agent was harried at best. The flight attendant was irritated and the cabin crew on my connecting flight to Atlanta was rude.

If it's true that front line employees treat customers the way their company treats them, Delta must be treating its employees very poorly. I feel sorry for them. I feel sorry for Delta, too, a once-great airline that sure isn't what it used to be. I feel sorrier for their passengers, many of whom don't seem to travel very often and probably don't know the difference. But I feel sorriest for Delta's frequent business travelers, the road warriors who each spend many, many thousands of dollars on airline travel every year. We deserve better.

We also know that what goes around comes around. We remember Eastern Air Lines, Elaine — and we have very long memories.

Your customers are very much like me, and like the young man I met at the Akron-Canton airport. They want to get their money's worth and they want to be treated well in the process. If they aren't, they will go somewhere else if they can.

This book will teach you innovative ways to provide sizzling customer service and why both service and delivery are necessary to exceed your customers' expectations. Between its covers you will learn to build your career by building a solid reputation for excellence by providing an environment of care, competence, and communication. And you will learn how to build your business by nurturing a front-line team that serves your customers' needs, wins their loyalty, and maintains long-term relationships of trust and confidence on your behalf.

After all, you are only as good as the last contact between your best customer and your worst front line employee. And your customers have very long memories.

Mike Stewart, CSP, is a performance development consultant and seminar leader who works with customer-centered companies that want to sell value, not price.

He authored/co-authored seven books. Mike is a Lifetime Medallion Member of Delta's frequent flyer club.

Chapter 1

Three Strategies for Establishing Legendary Customer Service

SAM BARTLETT

For several years before moving to Virginia, I attended a remarkable church in Orlando, Florida. It is so effective in executing its strategic plan, that it is visited and benchmarked as much by business leaders as by other parishes. What makes this church's success unique is the fact that it is in a terrible location, has inadequate facilities, and insufficient parking. The sanctuary is a converted skating rink. In spite of all these obstacles it attracts and retains hundreds of new *customers* every year and is one of the fastest growing churches in America. It has ten services per week just to accommodate everyone! How do they do it?

When you visit Northland Community Church you find out
that the leaders not only have a mission, but they actually
believe in their mission and implement it throughout the
organization. Attend any of the ten services, for example, and
no offering plate will be passed in front of you. This is quite a
shock to many who walk in with the underlying suspicion that
all most churches really want is money. Other visitors are
surprised to find so much ethnic diversity in attendance and on
staff. Still others are amazed when they can't locate the name of
the Senior Pastor on the attractive sign out front. He is
constantly saying, "No team member is more important than
any other team member," so he asked the board to remove his
name from the spotlight. Authentic actions like these generate
loyalty, commitment, and enthusiasm among church staff,
volunteers, and membership.

You have probably already guessed why this church is one
of the fastest growing churches in America — word of mouth.
Slick brochures, marketing campaigns and telemarketing are
conspicuous by their absence. All that you have read about
happy customers being your best marketers is true. The word on
the street about this church is that they are seeker sensitive or to
use business terminology, *customer friendly*. What are your
customers saying about your organization?

In order to build fierce loyalty and turn your customer base
into a marketing machine, you must establish what I call
legendary customer service. Customers need to believe deep
down that your organization actually believes in its mission to
put customers first. As more and more companies jump onto the
customer service bandwagon it actually becomes easier to spot
those who are merely giving lip service to customer service. I
advise clients not to create slogans or marketing campaigns
unless they are willing to back them up with authentic actions.
It is always better to *under promise and over deliver.*

Don't ask my parents to comment on Ford's slogan, *Quality is Job One.* They bought a Lincoln Continental that was a real lemon. The paint peeled, the engine blew, the sunroof leaked, the transmission failed… well, you get the picture. Despite the ribbing my father took from friends and family (I grew up in a small town where people follow NASCAR and are very opinionated about the best vehicle   on the road), his confidence in Ford never wavered. He had owned Fords all of his life and was confident that the company would stand by its product. After all, *Quality was Job One.* My mother wrote a letter to Alex Trotman, CEO. The generic response, in a nutshell, "Sorry for your troubles. We can't help." What did my parents do? It is still the gossip of this small town. My mom bought a Cadillac and my dad purchased a Dodge Ram pickup.

Contrast the reception my parents' letter got from Ford with how Nordstrom responded to an outrageous request from a writer/humorist pretending to be a customer (Letters from a Nut, Avon Books. 1997). Ted Nancy wrote a letter to Nordstrom's headquarters asking if he could buy one of their mannequins that looked just like his deceased neighbor. He wanted to present it to his neighbor's family as a sentimental gesture. Of course this wasn't normal policy and Nordstrom had never received a request like this one. Nevertheless, when you have a reputation for providing legendary customer service you find a way to put people over policy. Mr. Nancy received two heartfelt letters, one from Bruce Nordstrom, offering to locate and sell him the mannequin.

Does Ford care about customers? Of course they do. They have simply decided to go a different route than Nordstrom, Southwest Airlines, The Ritz Carlton, LL Bean, Northland Community Church, and others who have chosen to make their customer service *legendary*. The fact that you are reading this book already tells me that you want to make customer service a priority. Why not do a *little bit more* and make it legendary? In the next few pages I will describe three strategies that will help you do it.

Strategy #1 — Empower Employees So They Can Serve Customers in *Real Time*

When an employee is capable of meeting a need but has to wait for approval, both the employee and the customer are devalued. In order to be as productive as possible, I ask for a business upgrade when I check into a hotel. About 40% of the time the person behind the counter gives a quick response. More often than not, however, the sheepish reply is, "I can't do that Mr. Bartlett. You will need to speak to my manager." This is frustrating for the customer and embarrassing for the employee. I feel like going over to the manager and saying: "I am a consultant and people pay me to do seminars on effective leadership. If you don't mind, I would like to give you one for free." One of my clients, a utility company, has a great definition of empowerment.

> *Giving employees encouragement and visible permission to be creative in solving customer problems and making improvements in the way we do business.*

For this company empowerment is not a buzzword. Management empowers the employees by giving them three things — **information, training**, and **accountability**.

Most customer requests do not require a specialist. They require an employee who knows how to access information quickly. My local dental office has legendary customer service.

If you have a billing or scheduling question and cannot reach the bookkeeper, anyone on the team (including the hygienist) can access enough information to address your inquiry. No turf wars here! There is one word every employee knows never to use — the word *my*. Drs. Williams and Solberg continually cast the vision that it is not *my* patient or *my* desk or *my* work area — it is *ours*. Consequently, employees don't have to hoard information to protect their value to the organization.

Empowerment is not *abandonment*. I spend a lot of time with print shops and have a love/hate relationship with one of my suppliers. Sometimes I receive superior service and other times they mess up simple jobs. I am still rewarding them with business because I recently developed a friendship with one of their front-line employees. Dan takes care of me. The other workers are empowered as much as Dan. The problem is they don't know what they are doing. They have been sent out to serve customers without adequate training. To paraphrase Harvard business professor Leonard Schlesinger, *Most companies require little more than a pulse before they send employees out to interact with customers.* Dan received his expertise from a previous employer that took training seriously.

You can no longer consider your customer representatives as *entry-level* employees. They are your company's *ambassadors*. Since you are asking them to do more, you must invest more in their development. Training *is* expensive. But, have you stopped and evaluated the cost of not training? It costs over five times more to acquire a new customer than to keep an existing one.

Effective training starts with orientation. The impression a new hire receives during the first days on the job will drastically influence output for the remainder of his or her employment at your company. This is why Disney gives a summer part-timer more orientation training than most full-timers receive at other places. Disney's goal is to indoctrinate employees early on with a vision of being cast members to a crowd of customers who will leave not with a product, but a *memory*.

There is a huge debate today among training experts as to whether or not you can take someone with poor people skills and develop him into a customer service champion. Many claim that there is not much you can do with someone who has a crabby nature. Your best bet, they say, is screening and hiring people with what Daniel Goleman calls *emotional intelligence*. I agree with the importance of hiring the right people and have taught seminars on effective interviewing. On the other hand, I have seen too many lives transformed through high impact training to believe that people can't or won't change. If your training programs are not working, take a hard look at how they are being designed and delivered. A lack of accountability may be the real problem. Some people never change until they hurt enough that they have to change.

Empowered employees are not loose canons. Nor are they without links to your goals and expectations. You must *inspect* what you *expect* and reward those who are modeling your vision of providing legendary customer service. Many progressive organizations are now pegging pay to customer satisfaction. It frustrates your *best* customer service champions when team members are not pulling their weight and nothing is done about it. A new book (<u>From Worst to First: Behind the Scenes of Continental's Remarkable Comeback</u>, John Wiley & Sons, Inc. 1998), describes how CEO Gordon Bethune gave Continental's employees a *vision to become the best, measured the results* and *shared the rewards*. Now that's a formula for success! The kind of *real time* empowerment that I have been describing creates a triple win. The employee feels better about his or her job, turnover is reduced, and the customer gets better service.

Strategy #2 — Make Sure You Know What Your Customers *Really* Want

A good friend decided to defy the odds and open an independent Italian restaurant in South Florida. Effective marketing got customers in the door and the best bread in the galaxy kept them coming back. My wife and I visited his establishment soon after it opened and left saying, "The food is not bad, but the bread is heavenly." A year or so later I was in North Miami for a training session and made a surprise visit to Tony's restaurant. What I found was disheartening. The crowd was light and even worse *no more heavenly bread.* After dinner my friend expressed his concern as to whether or not he could keep the doors open. "What happened to your bread?" "Oh," he said, "the customers were eating so much of it that I was not selling many desserts. I decided to replace it with my current offering." "Hearing any complaints?" I pressed. "Yes, but this new bread is a lot healthier for you." I simply could not convince Tony that maybe there was a connection between the sudden drop of word-of-mouth growth and the surprise menu switch without customer input. As Coca-Cola found out with the *New Coke* debacle, *whoever brings the bat and ball makes the rules.*

Of course the only way to really find out the unique needs of your customers is to spend time with them via focus groups, phone surveys, written feedback, informal dialogue, and a host of other proven methods. Sears found out they could get more feedback by making the process quick, easy, and *rewarding.* Customers were offered an instant discount on an item they were purchasing if they would dial an 800 number and answer a few questions. The Don CeSar, like many hotels, sends out a letter soliciting feedback after your stay. The only difference (and the reason I respond promptly) is that the Don CeSar will enter my name into a drawing for an elaborate expense paid weekend.

As you keep your ear to the ground, two things will separate you from the crowd and move you from ordinary to legendary. First, make sure that your leadership spends a few hours every month on the front-lines interacting with customers and handling customer complaints. Senator Bob Graham continues to be one of Florida's most popular politicians. Our love affair with Bob started when he was governor and did something that earned him admiration from friends and foes. Once a month he would spend a day working (really working) alongside of front-line workers from various industries. His goal was to gain firsthand knowledge of the issues they faced and to express his appreciation for their contribution in making Florida great. Needless to say, his approval ratings soared. Want to send a powerful message to both your employees and your customers? Walk a mile in their shoes.

Secondly, draw upon the growing data from the Service Quality Movement as a framework for gathering feedback. We can thank Dr. Leonard Berry and others for giving us solid research on what customers' use to judge the quality of our service. This data is commonly referred to as the RRATE factors (Service Quality, Irwin Professional Pub.,1988). Most of your feedback from customers will fall into one of five categories.

Reliability — your ability to perform promised services *dependably and accurately*.

Responsiveness — your willingness to *help* customers and provide *prompt* service.

Assurance — the *knowledge* of your employees and their ability to convey *trust and confidence*. Assurance is reflected in the statement, "As long as I know you are worried about it, I don't have to worry about it."

Tangibles — the appearance of your physical facilities, equipment, personnel, and marketing materials.

Empathy — the way you provide *individual* service in a *caring manner.* Remember that people don't care how much you know, until they know how much you care.

The bottom-line, know your customers! Intuit is on top of the personal finance software market because they listen to customers. They have a program called *Follow Me Home* where they visit customers at home and observe them using their software. They then go back and design changes and upgrades based on firsthand observation and feedback. Sid Fulton Appliances, a small appliance and TV store in Paducah, Kentucky, was able to pick up the market share even after the high volume discount stores came into town by staying close to customers. People were willing to pay higher prices to know that they could pick up the phone, call Sid, and have a new washer installed by the time they got home from work. Sid is successful because he knows that *his* customers want more than an appliance, they want *convenience* and *peace of mind.* What do your customers *really* want?

Strategy #3 — Use Customer Complaints as an Opportunity to Shine

Most of your customers are themselves providing internal or external service at their place of employment. They know that you will not deliver perfect service 100% of the time. What they expect, however, is prompt resolution when problems arise. I encourage you to welcome complaints. They alert you to blind spots and give you an *opportunity to shine.*

My background is counseling and for several years I worked with married couples in trouble. I learned early that most people don't get along because they don't know how to get along. In a majority of cases the problem was an incompetence factor rather than an incompatibility factor. As one person put it, "When I got married I was looking for an *ideal*, ended up with an *ordeal*, now I want a *new deal*." Teach your employees how to handle agitated customers and they will stop avoiding them. A part of my intervention strategy with couples was to offer training on how to listen non-defensively, to speak up assertively, to handle conflict and manage anger, to give and receive constructive feedback, and a host of other people skills. These are the same skills that my business clients are utilizing to handle customer complaints in a positive manner.

Most complaints, incidentally, are about how a particular employee *treated* a customer. Once again it is a people skill issue. We have a tendency to react rather than respond to customer complaints. There are four reactions to avoid when dealing with an irate customer.

Don't Deny or Defend

When a customer complains, the initial issue should not be who is right or wrong. The first response should be one of empathy. "Thank you for bringing this to my attention," is a phrase that does not admit guilt and yet does not deny or defend. Remember, at least a complaining customer is still a customer.

Don't Minimize

Seventy percent of all anger is displaced anger. It should not surprise us that customers will sometimes make a mountain out of a molehill. They had to wait five minutes and attack you as if it was an eternity. Learn to depersonalize by realizing that they may be more upset at a spouse or the speeding ticket they got yesterday than you. "I am so sorry you had to wait; tell me what it is you need and let me see how I can help," is another example of an empathic response.

Don't Assume That the Customer Wants Something for Nothing

This world has its share of takers instead of givers. Nobody likes being taken advantage of. When employees become cynical about people, however, it will start showing up in both actions and attitude. Studies have shown that most disgruntled customers only want the *wrong righted and an apology*. They don't want you to give away the store. It may also cost more in the long run to process and drag out a customer request than to honor it unconditionally.

Don't Allow Customers to Verbally Harass You

Customer service reps must consider themselves professionals in the truest sense. They are called to serve, but not to be abused. Train them to be assertive communicators in the face of emotionally charged situations. I was scheduled to do a seminar in Springfield, Illinois. I got off the airplane late on a Thursday evening and couldn't find my hotel. It turns out I had flown to the wrong city. I was in Springfield, Missouri. I couldn't do anything that night except find a place to sleep and arrange for a 6:30 a.m. flight the next morning to Illinois via St. Louis. I made it to St. Louis, but they would not let me on the small plane to Springfield. I had a boarding pass, but could not find the actual ticket to go with it.

"Mr. Bartlett, we are pulling out of here in ten minutes. If I were you, I would go the main counter and see if you can get this taken care of before we leave." Have you ever been in a rush and felt like everyone else was moving in slow motion? I became a customer service rep's worst nightmare. "You have to get me on that plane," I shouted. "I have thousands of people waiting on me in Springfield" (I think 40 was the actual number). Have you noticed that when people lose control they tend to exaggerate the truth?

The person behind the counter then asked me about payment. I really lost it. "Payment!" "I will worry about payment six months from now. I will pay for it again if I have to. I've got to get on that plane!" At that moment this petite person (size has nothing to do with your ability to be assertive) looked up from behind the counter and made eye contact with me. I could read her eyes. They were saying, "I am a person of value. I am not going to allow you to verbally harass me." She then made a cushion statement just like I teach in my seminars on *Handling Difficult People*. "Mr. Bartlett, I would like to help you get on that plane. For me to help you get on that plane, you are going to have to be quiet and let me do my job." All I could say at that moment was, "Yes ma'am."

Providing legendary customer service does not mean that you allow customers to *undermine* your *front line*. I teach employees who serve customers over the telephone that it is okay to say to someone yelling obscenities in your ear, "I am eager to talk with you about this when we can discuss it in a constructive manner. I am hanging up now. Please call back when you are ready to talk." Let's review. The next time you come face to face with an irate customer don't defend, don't minimize, don't assume that he or she wants something for nothing, and don't allow verbal harassment.

One of my business partners, Lyman Baker, has a good friend whose children made straight A's all through high school and college. More than once he has been asked to share the secret of his children's academic accomplishments. His response illustrates the essence of this chapter.

> *When they were in middle school, every week or so I would ask them what it took to get a C, a B, an A. 'To get a C,' they would say, 'you have to show up and do the basic work. To get a B you have to do the basic work and a little more. To get an A you have to do the work, a little more, and then throw in some extra effort.' I would, at that point, remind my children that over 80% of their efforts were being expended just to get a C. Why not do the little bit more and get a B or an A?*

The difference between ordinary and extraordinary is the *little extra*. Dr. Janice Crouse, former speech writer for President Bush and my mentor, tells a powerful story about a business willing to do a little bit more.

> *When we celebrated our 25th wedding anniversary, we retraced our Smoky Mountain honeymoon trip. In spite of the fact that every place we visited knew that we were celebrating a special occasion, only one place did anything to note that fact. The Burning Tree restaurant in Gatlinburg gave us a special table and, at the end of our meal without silly fanfare, but rather with quiet dignity, brought us a decorated cake. We, of course, stop there anytime we are going through Gatlinburg and tell all of our friends about the Burning Tree Restaurant. They took a small, inexpensive extra step and turned an ordinary lunch into a special event.*

A seasoned executive from AT&T who travels internationally recently said this about staying at a Disney property. "When I checked into my room, I found a postcard with a picture of the hotel by the telephone. It was just like thousands of other postcards I had seen in hotels around the world. The only difference was that this card had a stamp on it. It was ready to mail. I was impressed!"

What does it cost to move from average customer service to legendary? Sometimes it could be as little as a few cents. Go ahead! Make your customer service legendary. Empower your ambassadors to make decisions, help them know your customer's needs, and train them to shine by professionally handling complaints. That's what *a little bit more* is all about.

Bio — Sam Bartlett

Sam Bartlett is a noted authority in the areas of team building, communication, conflict management, and how to provide legendary customer service. He has trained tens of thousands of people through public seminars and has provided on-site training for companies such as AT&T, Rockwell, Black & Decker, Johnson & Johnson and Mellon Bank. Participants consistently rank his workshops as "the best they have ever attended."

Sam has produced several popular training videos and is on the faculty of National Seminars Group, a division of Rockhurst College, and the Mayerson Academy for Human Resource Development. He currently serves as Managing Director for Alliance Performance, a consulting company, and as President of Sam Bartlett Seminars.

Contact Information:

Sam Bartlett Seminars
PO Box 1353 Galax, VA 24333
Toll Free: 1-800-513-5832
E-mail: Sam@sambartlett.com

Chapter 2

LIZ TAHIR

Getting Rid of the Rulebook

> *"The flexible man has many eyes to see his opportunities."*
>
> **MAHMOUD ZGHOBY**

One recent morning, at 10:35, I walked into McDonald's and ordered a sausage biscuit. The counter person turned around to look up at the clock. Then she said to me: "Breakfast ends at 10:30." A little surprised, I told her that it was only a few minutes after that time and couldn't she sell me a biscuit? She just stood there and repeated "We don't serve breakfast after 10:30."

What logic is there to selling a sausage biscuit at 10:29 a.m. and deliberately not selling that item six minutes later, simply because that is the "rule"? What does McDonald's do with leftover biscuits? Wouldn't it be more profitable to sell them? Or is there some sort of sausage biscuit heaven in the sky they all must go to when the clock strikes 10:30?

Now, McDonald's is a sharp, successful organization — the largest fast food operation in the world. And McDonald's, like all companies, needs policies to make its business run smoothly. And regulations must be set so employees know what the company expects of them. But does *common sense* go out the window? In this time of fierce competition and much talk of improving customer service, doesn't *judgment* on a one-to-one basis have a place?

After this experience, I started thinking about the rules and regulations we make as we run our business — rules that seem perfectly logical to us but totally illogical to our customers — rules that may even cause us to lose customers. I discussed this with several business colleagues and friends and every one of them had similar stories to tell, even one store owner who realized he was guilty, too!

Stories, Sad but True

The Furniture Purchase

Jean was moving into a new home, and went to a large furniture store in her city to shop for living room furniture. She selected items totaling $7,000. As the salesperson was writing up the sale, Jean stated she wanted the furniture delivered the next Friday, as she did not work on Friday and would be home that day to receive it. The salesperson consulted her delivery schedule and said Tuesday was the scheduled day for deliveries in Jean's neighborhood. No exceptions. After deciding she could stay home from work on Tuesday to await the delivery, Jean asked for a definite time. No, again. The salesperson said they never give definite times. But Jean could choose between 8 a.m. - noon or 1-5 p.m. (just like the utility company).

After thinking it over, Jean became exasperated and decided the company was just too difficult to do business with and she saw no need to give them her money. She told the salesperson to cancel the order. Now, faced with the loss of a $7,000 sale and a sizable commission, the salesperson quickly made a few calls to various levels of management. After 20 minutes of calls, the store agreed to deliver the furniture on Friday as requested.

But why put a $7,000 customer through all this to satisfy a "rule"? Shouldn't it be a no-brainer to say "yes" to a good customer's request?

Closing Time at the Cleaners

Jeff, the owner of a men's store, was going on a market trip Sunday and planned to pick up two suits from the cleaners on Saturday afternoon. Knowing the cleaners closed at 5:30, he left his business early in what he thought was time enough to get there. Well, slow moving traffic caused him to arrive at 5:40. The door was locked but he felt he was in luck as he saw the owner's car in the driveway and could see someone moving in the back of the shop. Though he kept loudly knocking on the door and calling to the person inside, there was no response. Jeff made the market trip without those suits, vowing never to trade with that cleaners again.

But this started Jeff thinking about his own store closing time and that he might also be guilty of the same rigid practice. Usually, he locked the doors exactly at the 6 pm closing then went to the office to tally up. The salespeople left by the back door and he wasn't far behind. So Jeff set a new "rule," one more customer-friendly. The official store closing time would still be posted as 6 pm. But the door would not be actually locked until 6:15. He felt the additional 15 minutes of time this cost him was worth it.

Contrast this cleaner's story with one that Mike, the bell captain at the Hotel Algonquin in New York City, told me about his experience in a new Nordstrom store that had just opened in his New Jersey neighborhood. Mike and his wife were looking around the store and stopped at the customer service counter to ask what time the store closed. The associate smiled and said: "Whenever you're finished shopping, sir." What a very customer-friendly answer! Mike and his wife felt like royalty. Doesn't Nordstrom have an official closing time? Of course. But apparently you won't get thrown out of the store with bells going off.

The Parking Ticket Saga

One of the downtown retailers has a parking garage in its building and offers 3 hours free parking with any same-day purchase in the store, no minimum amount. Since I had plans to meet a friend for lunch in a nearby restaurant, I parked in that garage. After lunch, I stopped in the store to buy some hosiery, then went to the service desk and had my ticket stamped, got in my car, and drove to my office.

Later in the afternoon I had an unexpected appointment near that same building, so I decided to move my car from my office to that garage. Since I knew I would be going home from there, I parked in the building again. When I finished my appointment after about an hour, I realized I could either pay the full $5.00 parking fee or buy something in the store again and get the ticket stamped. Sure, I would still be spending some money, but I would have something to show for it. So I purchased my favorite mascara (which I would usually have bought at another store). Then I was off to get my parking ticket stamped. But trouble was lurking in the winds. When I gave the serviceperson my sales check and ticket, she asked: "Weren't you in here earlier?" I said that I had been, and naively thought she was going to thank me for making another purchase. Instead I heard, "Sorry, the policy is only one stamped ticket per person per day." It took me a while to get that. Was she telling me that the company would rather I *not* come in but once a day? Would they rather I make only one purchase instead of two? Then shouldn't they have a guard at the door stamping hands so if a person tries to come inside the store more than once they can identify them? "Hey, you, what do you think you're doing, trying to sneak in here again? Out!"

Is the reason for the retailer offering a free-parking-with-purchase promotion to get people to spend time in the store and to make a purchase? Absolutely. So if an occasional customer comes in the garage/store twice, isn't that an advantage for the retailer?

Breaking These Rules

Could any of the following "Sorry, that's our policy" stories have taken place where you work?

1. *Rule: No food or drink allowed in the store.* Sally was shopping in a mall with her six-year-old son and decided to go in a favorite designer apparel store. She had purchased a soft drink for her son and forgot he was carrying it. When she entered the store, the salesperson came up to her and politely told her they did not allow food inside. Embarrassed, Sally apologized and left.

Few store owners like to contend with food and drink in their store so they post signs on the doors which are not offensive. But what *is* offensive is embarrassing anyone who walks in your store. Aren't all your efforts geared toward getting people to come in? Why would you deliberately throw them out? And how many times is it likely someone would walk in with food after seeing the sign on the door? Not many. So when it happens, just make an exception and say nothing (and hope the kid doesn't spill the drink). Suppose the kid comes in with a dripping chocolate ice cream cone? In that case, you might want to pleasantly say something like: *let me get you a napkin for that* (and then get the biggest one you can find!).

2. *Rule: The receiving dock closes at 4 pm.* The carrier drives up at 4:30 and is turned away. Whose merchandise is it that gets taken back and delivered the next day, wasting a day of selling time? Not the driver's. Why not close the receiving area at 4 but put a bell on the door so you can take in an *exceptional* delivery.

3. *Rule: No merchandise returned without a receipt.* If Mrs. Jones is an even occasional customer of your store and wants to return an item without a receipt, take it back with a smile and give her full credit. Unless you encounter some very extreme circumstances, it always pays to give customers the benefit of the doubt. How often do you get "taken" on such requests? Once a month? Once a year? Never enough to justify offending a customer.

4. *Rule: Make no exceptions to a promotional policy.* A local store was having a promotion: "Buy $75 in our fragrance department and receive a complimentary crystal vase." My purchase came to $72.75. I asked if I could have

a crystal vase. "Oh, I'm so sorry, but the purchase has to be $75." When I protested, I was told that "if we make an exception for you with that amount, we would have to do it for everyone who asks." (So?) I was annoyed with this rigid and unreasonable attitude and since I knew I could find the same brand in at least two other stores in town, I decided to go elsewhere to make my purchase.

Company policy should be to make a decision on a situation based on its own merits, never a blanket rule. Since I obviously felt strongly enough about this to cancel the purchase, wouldn't it have been better to please me by granting my request than to annoy me enough to leave the store? That store lost more than $2.25 that day with its no-exception rule. When the amount is within a few dollars of a promotion, exceptions could be made 1. when the customer specifically *asks* and 2. as a gesture of good will even when the customer does not ask. "Since your purchase is so close," the salesperson could say, "I'd like to give you a complimentary crystal vase for shopping with us." Choose to *delight* the customer at every opportunity you're given.

There is another lesson in this scenario: *the power of differentiation.* If this store had an exclusive on the fragrance label or something different about the offerings that I could not find anyplace else, they would have had me. They didn't. Whether you sell apparel, lumber, or insurance, the more you differentiate your company from the competition, whether in products or in services, the more you tie your customers to you.

5. *Rule: We can't be responsible for that.* John is largely confined to his home because of medical reasons. He orders a lot of merchandise by phone. He called one of the stores in town to buy a sweater recently advertised. He told the sales associate he was sending a taxi for the package and since he

knew the men's department was on the first floor, he requested the sweater be kept in the department. The taxi driver could park in the passenger zone for the few minutes it would take to pick up the package. But the salesperson told him they were not allowed to keep customer packages in the department so he could get it from the service desk upstairs. John said the driver would not have time to go up to that area and possibly have to wait, and could they please keep it in the department? "Sorry, our policy is that we can't be responsible for customers' packages in the department." It took 20 more exasperating minutes of John's time to locate and then repeat his story to the store manager before it was agreed the store could make an exception and honor John's request.

Was there really any need to put a customer through this ordeal? The policy of not keeping customer packages in the department is a reasonable one; not only is there a possibility for misplacement or damage, but packages left around the department add to the clutter. But when a specific request is made for a legitimate reason, an exception should be made and made quickly. There should be no reason for the associate to have to get permission from management.

6. *Rule: No seating in this section.* In a restaurant, a customer asks to sit in a favorite section. "Sorry, that section is closed until later." If the customer really prefers to sit in that section, why not make the customer happy and let her sit wherever she wants, as long as the table is not reserved and she understands she will be alone in the section? The wait staff will just have to walk a little farther. Allow for not only the preferences but the *eccentricities* of your customers!

7. *Rule: No seating until entire party arrives.* Dick and his friend drove to a new restaurant in Manhattan for dinner.

When they got to the restaurant, the driver let Dick out to go in to secure a table while he drove on to find a parking space. The restaurant hostess, however, had other ideas, for when Dick told her there would be two for dinner, she said he could not get a table until the other party arrived. So Dick waited. In the meantime, folks were beginning to come in. Fearing the restaurant was getting crowded, Dick again asked for a table, assuring the hostess his friend was obviously just having trouble finding a parking space. "Sorry, that's our policy." Then Dick got a brilliant idea. He went to the hostess and announced "Party of one!" He got a table.

I asked several of my restaurant-owner clients their opinion of this policy and all said that while some restaurants do this, it serves no purpose and is an arrogant way to treat customers.

Giving Employees Authority

What rules and regulations in your company have the potential for offending your customers? Certainly, it is necessary to establish policy and regulations to help your business run efficiently. But are these rules so rigid they have no exceptions?

When there is a need for an exception, your employees should not only be authorized but encouraged to use their judgment in each situation. Will employees bypass company rules, even knowing that doing so would better serve their customer, if they fear criticism or reprisal from management? Never! The fear of management criticism can paralyze your employees. Make sure your associates feel assured they can (and should) make decisions one-by-one to solve a customer's problem. It's said that Sam Walton, founder of Wal-Mart, ran his business on the precept that *no* decision is ever sacred.

Involve your employees in the decision making process as much as possible. Why? Because those who are charged with *implementing* policy must also have a voice in *making* that policy.

The employee handbook of Nordstrom's, the Seattle-based store group, consists of only one rule: *Rule #1: Use your good judgment in all situations. There are no additional rules.*

The reason Nordstrom's can feel comfortable having a one-rule policy for its employees is first, training, and second, trust. Part of that training is instilling the Nordstrom corporate culture in everyone, letting them know what is expected of them. Employees learn to do whatever it takes to make a customer happy. They are trained that Nordstrom's believes people in their store are *guests* and therefore *deserve* the best service. When employees are trained into this culture, they can produce the sales results they must achieve for success. The company will trust them with a lot of operational freedom in performing their jobs. However, if the employee has trouble buying into this culture, he will not stay employed at Nordstrom's.

Give the Lady What She Wants

Customers should never be aware of your rules. (Mr. Marshall Field was right when he said years ago: "Give the lady what she wants.") Whatever your rules and policies are, they should have no obvious impact on your customers. Each situation should stand on its own. If you find you are having to make too many exceptions, well, then you have a bad regulation and it should be changed! Common sense and good judgment should "rule" every time.

Debunking an Old Rule

We couldn't talk about getting rid of the rulebook without discussing the rule that many companies run their business on: *Treat all customers the same.*

All customers are entitled to your best efforts, aren't they? All customers are created equal, right? Well, no and no. In today's competitive environment, that kind of thinking could put you out of business.

The focus today should be on relationship building with your best customers, not all your customers. Identify and satisfy your current customers. It is costly for any company to focus primarily on spending money trying to attract new customers. It is much more profitable to do more business with the customers you have. Do you really want all the customers you can get? No. You want to attract and keep the customers that are going to be more meaningful to your success.

Many companies know more about their products than about their customers. Sales-driven organizations view a sale as a culmination. Marketing-driven organizations (which you want to be) view a sale as an opportunity to build a relationship with that customer. These companies see the sale as a beginning, not an end. It is essential in today's competitive environment to maintain a customer database that allows you to know everything about your best customers: Family, lifestyle, preferences, purchases, etc. Then you can target your efforts specifically to each customer by maintaining meaningful contact with them. Build and differentiate your products and services for these customers rather than constantly working toward acquiring new customers. When you do this, you bond these customers to you. Loyalty doesn't come from merely satisfying customers; it comes from building an emotional partnership with them.

You think that logic drives sales? Rarely. What does drive sales is trust, respect, comfort... all attributes of a *relationship*.

No company can develop this with every customer. It is wasteful to use these efforts on customers who do not meet established criteria. Certainly every customer deserves to be treated in a respectful and civil manner. But what we are talking about here is giving your best customers special treatment, more services. Let them know constantly that you value their business and you want to continue to serve them for years to come.

Summary

A. Look at your policies through your customers' eyes. Review every rule and regulation in your company to see how your customer is affected by it. If a policy has the potential for adverse effect on your customers, change it or get rid of it entirely.
B. Customers should never be aware of your rules.
C. Authorize and encourage your employees to make decisions that will best serve their customers.
D. Teach your associates that exceptions can be made to rules. Recognize that every decision should be made on its own individual merits, not on a blanket policy.
E. Make your primary goal to do more business with the customers you have and a secondary goal to attract new customers.
F. Focus on building relationships with your best customers. Strive for emotional partnerships.
G. Break a few rules!

> *"If you obey all the rules, you miss all the fun."*
> KATHARINE HEPBURN

Bio — Liz Tahir

Liz Tahir grew up learning about customer service every day in her father's grocery store in the small Delta town of Tchula, Mississippi. She began her retail training at Neiman-Marcus Company, when the legendary merchant Stanley Marcus was at the helm. She continued her retail career, becoming vice-president of merchandising for D. H. Holmes Company, a four-state regional department store group headquartered in New Orleans.

In 1990 she established Liz Tahir & Associates, a marketing and management consulting firm. Though the company is based in New Orleans, Liz works internationally. As a consultant, she helps small and large companies, in such areas as marketing strategy, company branding, management skills, customer service, employee training. As a professional speaker, she gives sessions to associations and businesses on marketing, merchandising, negotiating skills, customer satisfaction, leadership development. She has been written about or quoted in numerous national publications including The Wall Street Journal & Inc. magazine and is a contributing editor for the Fairchild WWD/DNR Business Newsletter.

In 1996, Liz was named *Woman Business Owner of the Year* by the Woman Business Owners Association of New Orleans. She is a recipient of the Lifetime Achievement Award from the Fashion Group International, Alpha Region. She has been selected as a Role Model by the YWCA.

She is a member of the National Retail Federation, American Marketing Association and National Speakers Association. Liz is listed in Who's Who of Finance and Industry and Who's Who of American Women.

Contact information:
201 St. Charles Avenue
Suite 2500, New Orleans, LA 70170 USA
Phone: (504) 569-1670
Toll Free: (800) 506-1670
Fax (504) 524-7979
E-mail: liztahir@websiteventures.com

Chapter 3

MARK ROSENBERGER

Swing with Your Trapeze Buddy

"Hey, you caught me! Just the way you said you would! We're flying through the air with the greatest of ease!"

Does this describe your life with the people you count on most, or are you spending much of your time picking yourself up off the concrete after being dropped?

If you're being caught more and dropped less, then you're working like Trapeze Buddies. If you fall way too much, this will be the tool you've been looking for!

The metaphor of the Trapeze Buddy conveys the idea of teamwork, communication, precision timing and the *extra effort mentality*. The concept clearly conveys the grave consequences of someone not coming through as promised.

They're dropping you as you count on them to complete a task, function or provide information so you can do your job.

The Metaphor

I remember going to the big top circus with my parents. We nervously awaited the flying trapeze artists who would dazzle us from high above the arena floor. The talented artists jumped, flew, spun and caught one another with precision, often times, only inches from disaster. The rare times they missed, I let out a gasp in horror watching my circus hero tumble to the safety net below. I'm willing to bet they planned some of the falls just for effect. Believe me, it worked!

The Trapeze Artist:

What a perfect analogy for each of your jobs! Everyday you climb the ladder, stand on the platform and then swing out toward the middle. The entire time, what are you hoping will happen? The answer is obvious: at a predetermined, agreed upon time, someone from the other side will swing out and catch you!

Yet how many times have you climbed the ladder, stood upon the platform, swung out toward the middle only to hear some lame excuse like: "I wanted to have that information for you." "I TRIED to get it done on time." "We ALMOST have it complete." "The computer went down!"? It really doesn't matter what the excuse happens to be, you know the outcome. You're already spinning in the air because you're counting on someone to come through and now, once again, you've been dropped. Oh, and by the way, in most businesses there are no safety nets. In fact, at your place of work there are probably spikes sticking up! And you're heading toward them, fast!

We can glean many insights from the circus artists and apply key learnings to our real world work situations. Exploring the Trapeze Buddy model enables you to discover new insights and enhance team performance. Your internal customers (Trapeze Buddies) are counting on you to come through and catch them as they swing out and spin from their trapeze bars. Understanding the principles used by our circus examples will assist in the goal of being caught more and dropped less. Let's face it, we're all tired of being skewered and welcome the opportunity to be caught.

Use this chapter to guide you and your team through a **five-step** process creating a new perspective and set of skills that will result in you being caught more and dropped less.

Step I: What's in It For Me?

The first step in the process is to ask and answer the question: "What's in it for me?" Great question! What might be in it for you, your team and the company if you could count on being caught more and dropped less?

Why ask this question? The Answer: When everyone on the team understands the benefits of playing together at this new level, they more willingly participate. Conversely, if this question is not addressed and people see this new process as *the new flavor of the month*, there will be increased resistance and diminished positive results.

The benefits of a new Trapeze Buddy perspective include:

- Less stress on the job
- More proactive time, less reactive time
- Fewer problems and complaints
- Improved morale
- Reduced employee turnover
- Growing revenue & increased profits
- Improved customer loyalty
- Enhanced repeat business
- Increase in referrals
- Increased fun on the job
- Reduced headaches and hassles
- Job security
- Happier customers
- Increased productivity
- Decreased reworks
- The ability to attract and hire the best people

WOW! That's quite a list.

Are any of these benefits of interest to you? If you answered an enthusiastic "YES," you'll immediately see the benefits of applying the Trapeze Buddy model to your world. List three "Personal Benefits (PB's)" important to you. Use the above ideas to create your "PB's" and draw from additional life experiences.

What's In It for Me: "Personal Benefits" List: (Write PB's Here)

1. _____
2. _____
3. _____
4. _____
5. _____
6. _____
7. _____
8. _____
9. _____
10. _____

Step II: Trapeze Buddy Defined

Simply stated, a **Trapeze Buddy is "anyone you count on, or rely upon to complete a task, a function, or provide you with information so you can get your job done."**
Can you think of anyone who meets this definition? Most likely, plenty of folks come to mind. But don't stop there because conversely, **a Trapeze Buddy is "anyone who counts on <u>YOU</u> to complete a task, a function, or provide <u>HIM</u> with information so he can get <u>HIS</u> job done**." Even more people should come to mind using this expanded definition!

We are interdependent. Every day you count on dozens of people to come through so you can accomplish your mission. Conversely, dozens of people are counting on YOU to come through so they can accomplish their responsibilities.

Trapeze Buddies are inside and outside your organization. Peek again at the definition: "…anyone you count on or they count on you!" This definition includes vendors, suppliers, co-workers and even the customer.

It includes people in management, the front lines and even the behind the scenes folks. It takes into account the obvious people and the not-so-obvious people of every organization. The definition also includes family and community members. You have LOTS of Trapeze Buddies.

The definition is important because in one form or another it touches everyone in the organization. No one can say he's "just a… ". There are no "just a's". We're all Trapeze Buddies to someone!

Everyone counts and everyone makes a contribution… or should make a contribution.

Try this: Copy the definition and place it around the office as a constant reinforcement of the concept.

Step III: Trapeze Buddy Mind Mapping

You've discovered you have lots of Trapeze Buddies. Many have come to mind as you've considered the definition. The next step is to list all your Trapeze Buddies on paper. The process is called Mind Mapping. It'll help you clearly see your many interdependent Trapeze Buddy relationships.

Mind Mapping

The process is simple: Using the diagram on the following page, place your name in the center circle. Each of the circles surrounding your name represents a person, department or company that is your Trapeze Buddy. Notice the arrows in the diagram go in two directions. Why? Most likely, you're counting on one another and are interdependent. Your job is to list all your Trapeze Buddies, inside and outside the organization. Look for the obvious and the not-so-obvious. You will need more circles than the diagram offers, so draw lines and create more circles. The game is to discover and list as many Trapeze Buddies as possible. For those people attempting to take a short cut, it does not count to write "Everyone in the Company" or "Everyone in the Universe" on your list. You'll benefit by taking the time to create and diagram your Trapeze Buddies. The entire team should take several minutes and individually map out their partners.

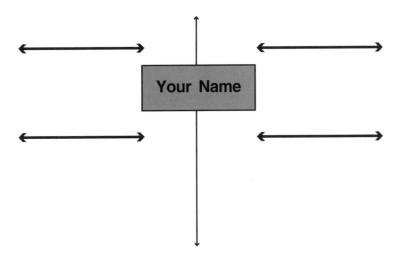

Figure 1

Next, review your findings with people on your team. The goal is to identify as many Trapeze Buddies as possible. One person in the group simply reviews the Trapeze Buddies they discovered. The rest of the group listens, and if they hear a Trapeze Buddy they can add to their list; they write it down. Each person debriefs his findings. Your list should include more Trapeze Buddies after this exercise.

My "Most Important" Trapeze Buddies

Place a *star* next to the three to five Trapeze Buddies you feel are *most important* to your success. Now, I know they're all important but for the sake of a future exercise, you'll want to narrow the scope to 3 - 5. *Important* can have several meanings. For example, you interact with a Trapeze Buddy frequently;

therefore, you feel he's important. It could be the person, who, if he drops you it really hurts and takes a long time to clean up and recover. Place a star next to his name.

Review your Trapeze Buddy Mind Map

Do you see several opportunities to be dropped? Did you include family members, friends and community responsibilities? Did you include the phone company, copier repair person and overnight delivery service? Hopefully, you've listed the receptionist, and the cleaning service for your home or office. As you proceed through your week you'll notice additional Trapeze Buddy Relationships. Write them down, grow your list. The game is to mind map all our Trapeze Buddy relationships. You'll be impressed with the number of critical relationships.

Step IV: Trapeze Buddy Success Distinctions

It's now time to design our game plan for being caught more and dropped less. We'll begin the process by exploring "HOW" real Trapeze Buddies interact with one another in a state of *heighten awareness*. Their lives are literally at risk! Understanding the subtle differences and uniqueness is to understand the *distinctions* between Trapeze Artists.

A distinction is defined as:
1. The condition of being different; difference.
2. What makes or keeps distinct; quality, mark, or feature that differentiates.

The Objective

The objective of this step is to answer two questions:
1. What can we learn and apply from the circus performers to our world?
2. What are the distinctions our circus hero's use that will work in our environment?

The Process

The following process will assist in understanding Trapeze Artist success distinctions. Your entire team (this is a great group exercise) has been designated as the official Trapeze Buddy *coaches* at your place of business. Your job is to study our circus performers. Based on your findings you will then provide coaching to your team about how to be caught often and dropped less. For example, you have a new hire who comes to the team. The new employee will learn the ropes sooner or later, we hope. Later can be very painful and expensive. So, from day one, you're going to provide coaching that will enable the new hires to perform at a high level with their new Trapeze Buddies. What will you tell them? How will you coach them? The answers will most likely come from the Trapeze Artist Success *distinctions* you've discovered.

Begin here: What's critical to two Trapeze Artists' putting on a successful show? What attitudes, behaviors, skills and levels of performance need to be in place to ensure a successful performance? As you put yourself in the performer's tights, you'll notice yourself asking: "What needs to be in place for the two of us to perform at a high level?" The answers to this question are your clues.

Allow me to prime the pump with an example of a Trapeze Buddy Success Distinction: **Communication**.

Your team discovers *communication* as being an attitude, behavior or skill needed to perform at a high level. Excellent! It makes sense that Trapeze Artists must communicate to put on an awesome show. So you place the word *communication* on the list of coaching ideas. BUT WAIT! You cannot stop by simply writing the word communication. We're looking for the distinctions that allow Trapeze Artists to perform at a high level. We want to understand how they might communicate differently than we do. We want to understand the *distinctions* of communication in order to enhance our own performance. After all, each of us communicates at work everyday! Some more effectively than others.

After listing *communication* on our coaching chart, we look for the high performance distinctions. For example, communication can be in the form of a monosyllabic grunt. Is this the type of communication used by our Trapeze Artists? You can bet your paycheck it isn't! Trapeze Artists communicate at a high level with heighten awareness. They communicate with *precision*. They recognize that a major cause of being dropped is from poor communication. A misunderstanding, assumption, or missed detail can be deadly! Given this insight, what are the distinctions of effective communication? How will you coach the new hire on the skill of communication?

Our Trapeze heroes would offer the following insights. The distinctions of communications include:

Precision. It's void of slop, fluff or play-it-safe terms. It's **timely** — you don't want to tell me an important detail after I'm already in the air spinning. Communication is **accurate** and **complete**. Trapeze artists incorporate three communication keys: **Verify, clarify** and **confirm**. Let's explore these items in more detail to glean additional insights.

Verify: These are illustrations of questions used to verify: Airlines, rental car companies and hotels are notorious for *missing communications* and dropping details. It can make for a long, painful experience if I fail to verify the communication. Does everyone have the same understanding of the communication? Are expectations in agreement? Has the timing been double checked? Does everyone understand their roles and responsibilities in the process? I travel a lot. I've learned after being dropped many times that I need to verify details and information. Compile a check list of items that would benefit from verifying in your organization. Try this: One powerful verifying technique is to ask a Trapeze Buddy to feed back to you his understanding of your communication. You'll know immediately if your communication was received in the manner intended!

Clarify: Based on the verifying technique described above, you'll know very rapidly if your communication is on target. If communication is uncertain or confused, now is a great time to insert clarity. Spend a few extra minutes on the front end of a communication to verify and clarify. It will literally save you and your team hours of headaches, hassle and trauma on the back end. The key to precision communication is not the fact you said something, but rather did your Trapeze Buddy *get it*. Was there understanding in the manner intended? That's precision communication. Of course if they don't *get it* now's the time to add clarity.

Confirm: A win-win strategy for Trapeze Buddies is to confirm agreements and deadlines *before* they are due. Why wait until it's too late to remind, reinforce or confirm an important issue, or deadline with the people you count on most? If you're playing for win-win results there is no reason why you wouldn't confirm and confirm early. If you're waiting *to see if they come through,* you're playing a game other than win-win. Our objective here is to minimize the chances of being dropped and maximize the opportunities to be caught. A friendly reminder can save countless hours of headaches and hassles.

Try this: Gain agreement with Trapeze Buddies that you will support one another with important time lines and reminders. Time activate reminders far enough in advance so people can come through and accomplish what they promised as agreed. Confirming will be a useful tool for all Trapeze Buddies.

Additional Success Distinctions

You've listed communication with several corresponding distinctions as an important success distinction. What additional attitudes, skills, behaviors and performance standards will your new hire and Trapeze Buddies need to understand before they can perform effectively together? Your team puts their creative minds together and someone offers: **Timing.** Excellent! Is timing important to our circus friends? You bet it is! And is timing important in your business or industry? Count on it! Customers have expectations. Co-workers have expectations. Timing is essential to the successful, smooth operation of every business.

The next step is to define the distinctions associated with timing for your organization. We're helping the team understand exactly what timing means. Does it mean answer the phone in three rings, or return calls within three hours or have the document to you by a certain time? What does timing mean in your organization? Don't assume the new hire (or anyone else on the team for that matter) understands what the timing issues are in your organization.

Try this: Map out the key timing issues critical to your company's success. What are the performance standards associated with timing? Create a handout that helps the new hires see and understand the critical timing issues in your organization. Detail their participation and responsibility in the timing processes. Use this "Timing Sheet" as a tool to ensure Trapeze Buddy success.

One more timing reminder: If for some reason you won't be able to come through on an agreement as promised, for goodness sakes, let your Trapeze Buddies know **before** they leap off the platform and begin spinning! They'll have many more choices and options with their feet on the ground rather than in mid air. Once they're in mid-air the choices are limited to choices like: face down or face up on the concrete? Both options hurt!

Take time to add more ideas to the Trapeze Buddy Distinctions for Success profile now.

Trapeze Buddy Distinctions for Success

Profile:

Success Criteria	Performance Distinctions	Priority
1. Communication	Verify, Clarify, Confirm. Precision, Accurate Complete, Timely.	
2. Precision Timing		
3.		
4.		
5.		
6.		
7.		
8.		
9.		
10.		

Figure 2

You've worked with your team to create Trapeze Buddy Success Distinctions. You are now able to communication with other Trapeze Buddies about needed distinctions for success.

You're able to speak to all Trapeze Buddies in specific terms about how they can contribute to the overall success of the organization. The entire team can work at further refining the performance so no one gets dropped! This is a powerful tool if used with the entire team. You're ready to take the game to the next level: designing a Trapeze Buddy Report Card.

Step V: The Trapeze Buddy Report Card

The premise here is simple: Trapeze Buddies and customers walk around with mental report cards scoring your performance every day! Customers are evaluating your performance based on the criteria most important to them. Trapeze Buddies have needs to insure success. If you score an "A" on these high criteria topics, you enhance the opportunity of being caught more often.

There are score cards being used in many situations every day. A classic example is with "significant other" relationships! I'm well aware my wife has a mental score card titled: "This is How I Know Mark Loves Me." I'm learning that if I score an "A" on the topics most important to her, I get to sleep indoors! I'm also aware that if I do what's on her score card but don't perform in the manner desired, I'll be sleeping outside. An example is in order: I know a major, high criteria topic on her score card is to be told I love, adore and appreciate her. And, she wants to be told often!

Now, do I need to tell her *just right* that I do in fact love, adore and appreciate her? You know I do. If I come home feeling mad, bent out of shape, irritated and moody and a snooty tone comes out as I rudely say, "Love You!" do I score any points? You know I don't score points. In fact, I'm willing to bet I've lost points and I'll be sleeping outside. There are several additional items on my wife's score card. If I score an

"A" on the entire list, who wins? We both win!

Trapeze Buddies have report cards as well. There are items they need from you and others to perform their job brilliantly. The Trapeze Buddy Report card will help identify the win-win elements needed by each partner.

Look at the sample report card. Select one important Trapeze Buddy and place his name on the top line. Down the left column, write the topics, issues, attitudes, behaviors or performance standards needed by this particular Trapeze Buddy. Answer the question: "What does this person need from **me** in order to perform their job brilliantly?" Jot your ideas down the left-hand column.

Once you've completed the exercise, push for a PLUS 10% improvement. Ask your Trapeze Buddy to verify and confirm, delete from and add to the list. Your goal is to create a clear picture of how to win with your Trapeze Buddy. Your Trapeze Buddy should be doing the same activity for you: what do you need, from him, to perform your job brilliantly? Together, you're creating a win-win relationship by gaining a clear understanding of what's most important to both of you. Complete this exercise with your five, ten or 100 most important Trapeze Buddies. You'll be amazed at the positive impact.

Try this: You created a list of Trapeze Buddy Success distinctions. Can any of these be added to The Trapeze Buddy Report Card? Make sure your report cards include items such as professionalism (whatever that means in your industry), accuracy, completeness, timeliness—all essential trapeze Buddy elements.

Trapeze Buddy Report Card

Name of Trapeze Buddy: _____

Success Distinction   Priority   Performance

Figure 3

Answer: "What does this person need from <u>me</u> to perform his job brilliantly?"

By taking your team through the five Trapeze Buddy steps you'll be on your way to being caught more and dropped less. But a word of caution: just like the circus counterparts, the process will require practice. Plenty of practice!

Once you get the hang of swinging together, you'll be pleasantly surprised with the amazing show you'll put on with your Trapeze Buddies. You'll hear people shouting: "Hey, you caught me! Just the way you said you would! We're flying through the air with the greatest of ease!" Keep swinging!

Bio — Mark Rosenberger

Mark Rosenberger is the Founder and Director of WOW! Performance Coaching, Inc. As a professional speaker and consultant, Mark shares ideas, concepts and strategies with corporations, associations and professional groups in Canada, the United States, Mexico and South America, blending his messages with passion, humor and contagious enthusiasm.

His approach is simple — Don't confuse the situation with razzle-dazzle theory but rather discover ideas you can use today to make a difference — and let's have fun doing it!

His extensive background provides an unparalleled perspective. His experience includes: education, sales and sales management, senior management, entrepreneur, consultant, innovator, author, husband, father and being Smokey-the-Bear for the Special Olympics.

Equally important to Mark's experience and his accomplishments: He has created and designed several training programs currently used in schools and corporations across America, including: **The Customer Loyalty System, Team Selling, How to Stay Sane in an Insane World, Tele-Consulting, The Service Audit, Service University! and Trapeze Buddies: How to be caught more often and dropped less often by the people you count on most.**

He has written dozens of articles focusing on customer service, teamwork and performance enhancement issues. His new book: **The PLUS 10% Game: 52 High Impact Leverage Points to Enhance Sales, Customer Loyalty and Teamwork** is being used by organizations to improve performance and team involvement in the success process. He is a candidate for the National Speakers Association Certified Speaking Professional designation and is an Ad Hoc Professor at the Management Institute, University of Wisconsin-Madison.

Contact Information:
WOW! Performance Coaching, Inc.
10680 Loire Avenue, San Diego, CA. 92131
Phone: (619) 578-7900
Fax: (619) 578-7065
E-Mail: wowseminar@aol.com

Chapter 4

MEG CROOT

Service Fundamentals

Introduction

Businesses today are charged to do less with more and to meet the increasing expectations of customers. Is it possible? The answer is a resounding YES when simple solutions and common sense strategies are employed as part of the day to day operation and culture.

Many businesses focus on the aspect of facilities that are highly themed, ornate, unusual or expensive. Is bigger better and does spending lots of money on bricks and mortar, unique features and bells and whistles guarantee a successful operation? Not always. Think of a time when you had a memorable service experience that made you feel good and want to share with others the nice time you had. Did it have more to do with how you were treated or the four walls and décor of a place?

The benefits of offering unexpected service include building customer loyalty and repeat business. Delightful service results in great public relations through word of mouth stories shared by satisfied customers. A direct result to the bottom line is increased revenues. Certainly, to command a premium price for services or products carries the expectation of exceptional service. Since good service gains a 6% market share per year and poor service loses a 2% market share per year, it makes sense to focus on the good service aspect of business.

The most valuable resource is time. A company's competition is anyone or anything else that competes for the customer's time. Put in these terms, it is clear how service that is fun and surprisingly good brings back customers. Creating experiences that involve and enthuse the customer is what makes a difference. From the standpoint of employees, providing customer pleasing service brings personal satisfaction and reward and makes work a more fun place to spend all day. When viewed in these terms, the value of a smile is clear!

Service Starts with People who Care

Begin by focusing on the most important element of service delivery — the service providers of your organization. All the good intentions, operational systems and gimmicks in the world won't overcome the bad feeling a customer gets from someone they encounter with a bad attitude. Never underestimate the power of your people. Ultimately, it is the individual interaction between a customer and a service provider that provides a pleasant and memorable experience. As noted by Dion Strachan, an executive of Atlantis Resort and Casino, "Put the right people in the job and everything else falls into place."

It sounds simple and it is simple. Hire the right people, manage the obstacles to great service in your operation and do the things that keep your team motivated and willing to work for your organization. Remember that the most valuable resource anyone has is his or her time. Make sure your employees feel good about spending their work time at your place of business and enjoy their job. These are the most critical steps you can take to increase the levels of customer service and maintain a culture that is focused on customer care.

Hiring the Right Stuff

Our neighborhood mailman has the right stuff. I have often observed him stopping to chat with the elderly gentleman up the street, taking time to say hello and show he cares. He always comes to the door when we receive a package too big for the box. I don't know his name, but I know he cares and I find that delightful.

Hiring the right people is a matter of identifying the traits and characteristics that are desirable in your ideal service providers. An easy way to do this is to look at someone in your organization who consistently receives excellent comments from customers and who is respected by his peers. Write down the behaviors and personality characteristics of this individual. Your list describing an excellent service provider might include descriptions like:

- Positive attitude
- Shows empathy and sympathy to customers
- Cares about details
- Good listener
- Enthusiastic
- Fun / playful personality
- Likes work
- Knowledgeable
- Friendly
- Helpful
- Flexible
- Efficient in delivering service
- Dependable

When hiring, identify people who are like your ideal. Test them with questions and role-plays that elicit responses and give an idea of how they would handle service situations and customer complaints. Keeping the emphasis on these qualities instead of basing a hiring decision primarily on education and experience will help identify star service providers. Conduct panel interviews that include the supervisor, someone from Human Resources, a peer or co-worker and someone from another department who will interact with the potential new team member. Finally, don't forget to really check references and ask questions that will give you a good idea about the individual you are hiring.

Watch for good eye contact and a confident friendliness during the interview, especially before and after they are in the "hot seat." The behavior shown before or after an interview is often more telling than what is observed during the questions.

Be sure to share honest information about the job and working conditions so the individual doesn't start a job that doesn't match his perception about what he was hired to do.

A little creativity in the interview also helps. Try tossing a ball to the interviewee and see how they respond. Are they surprised, flustered or do they react with delight and get into a playful mood? Customers often toss unexpected "balls" in the way of your staff. It's good to know how they handle a surprise. Another strategy is to give the interviewee a blank business card and ask them to write their name and fill in their anticipated title in three years. Look for people who would like to be in a customer contact position for the long term. If everyone you hire is just trying to move up the ladder to management, you will end up with a team of people who have an agenda other than customer care. It is always preferable to balance a team with people who are customer oriented with those who are ambitious for control.

Another strategy is to watch for times when you personally receive great service. Your next star employee may currently be someone else's star employee! There is nothing wrong with complimenting someone who gives excellent service and leaving your business card if they are interested in a "career opportunity!" Don't be afraid to assess their interest in working with you. In addition to looking for staff at other businesses, you may find ideal people in clubs, churches, volunteer associations and in the neighborhood. Keep your eyes open and remember to look for people who match your list of ideal characteristics.

It is more effective to spend your resources in hiring people with the "right stuff" than to spend energy trying to manage hiring mistakes. The right team gives continuity to your

business, helps build customer loyalty, reduces time and
money spent on hiring new workers continually and makes
your business a fun place to be.

Manage Obstacles, Not People

Management strategies and theories come and go as
quickly as an ice cream "flavor of the day." After a while, you
realize you can't really *manage* people. People have a mind of
their own, priorities, needs, personal problems and hidden
agendas that you can not always take into account. What you
do have control over is the *systems, resources and policies* that
make up your business.

Often it is these very systems, resources (or lack of) and
policies that create barriers to service for the customer. On a
recent shopping excursion to an outlet mall, I was ready to
spend several hundred dollars on a new wardrobe. Gathering
up an armful of bargains, I headed to the dressing room to
make my selections. I was stopped by an employee who said,
"I'm sorry, you can only have three items in the dressing room
at a time." This policy was written to minimize loss and theft.
Yet it severely hampered my ability to put together a couple of
new outfits. The employee did not offer any alternatives to the
rule or offer to help me by bringing new items in after I had
tried on the first three. I left in frustration without spending any
money. Think about your policies and how they impact your
customers. Are you punishing all of your customers because of
a fear of what a minority may do?

The best way to identify barriers to service is to listen to
your employees' requests. Barriers may include a lack of
equipment or supplies, training issues, inefficient procedures
or outdated policies. Involve your entire service team in

solutions for removing obstacles. How often are you saying *no*? Could you turn *no* to *yes* with a few changes? Get in the habit of saying *yes* and see what happens. If you practice this strategy, you'll find your staff starts to model it with their customers, finding ways to say *yes* instead of making excuses about having to say *no*.

Make a habit of daily shift meetings to hear employees' issues and to get an idea of what customers are saying. Ask things like:

> *"What do you need in order to do a better job for the customer?"*
> *"What have you done to make a customer really happy?"*
> *"What services or products do the customers want that we don't offer?"*

You will not only learn about any obstacles, you may discover ways employees are using creative solutions to satisfy and delight customers. This sharing will become a part of your organization's culture and encourage keeping the customers' needs in focus.

Create a Motivational Environment

Because what motivates your staff is so highly individual and personalized, it makes it hard to determine how you can inspire and motivate your staff to provide outstanding service. Successful customer focused organizations have discovered that by hiring people who care and managing obstacles, their employees perform at a peak most of the time. While it is difficult to continually "motivate" people, you can create an environment that is conducive to outstanding service and high levels of performance.

The best way to sustain a high level of service and a maximum performing team is to create a business that is desirable as a place of employment. Be the place everyone wants to work by thinking of your employees as "customers." What basic needs do they have in way of salary, benefits, needs for growth and recognition? What can you do to insure their comfort and enjoyment of coming to work for you each day? How can you delight your staff?

Encourage an environment and culture that is happy and fun. Allow for play as part of the job. Reward individual and team performance in creative ways. Look for times that socializing and team building can take place. Be flexible with work schedules and encourage creativity and innovation within your organization. Be a manager who cares about your team, and you are guaranteed to have a team that cares about customers. Think of good service in terms of creating two smiles; one on your customer's face and one on your employees'. The smiles are contagious and so is great service!

Common Sense Service Strategies

You know the value of a smile. You've hired the right people and you are managing them well. How can you be sure your customers will be given excellent service every day?

It is critical to create basic guidelines for the way you do business. This does not have to be complex or an all-inclusive list of how to handle every situation. In fact, the more simplified your guidelines are the easier it will be to train and make them part of your service culture. The oft-repeated example of making service simple is the content of the Nordstrom's Employee training manual. It reads, "Use your good judgment in all situations. There are no additional rules." The best part of this strategy is that it gives employees credit for having common sense and good judgement. If you've hired the right stuff, then you can be confident about having such a loosely defined policy with customer care.

Common Sense Rule #1

The Golden Rule of Service: *do not service unto others as you would be serviced unto, but service unto others as they wish.* Determine your customers' needs and expectations and fulfill them consistently. Make allowances for individual needs and preferences amongst your customers. Be sensitive to differences in ages and families (cultures, values, and religion.) Listen to your customers through formal surveys, collect comment cards, set up focus groups and ask for informal feedback on a daily basis. Use the information you gather for determining how to best provide the services and products your customers require.

Common Sense Rule #2

Get the basics right or nothing else you do matters. On a recent business trip, I needed lunch delivered to my room while working on a project. I ordered a salad and iced tea. The order was taken efficiently by a friendly voice. It arrived within 20 minutes delivered by a personable server who chatted with me briefly before leaving. As I started to enjoy my lunch, I realized that utensils, napkin and salad dressing were missing. The basics had been overlooked.

Consider the following to be basic customer care for any business:

Fulfill customer requests completely. Smile. Be clean. Be safe. Have fun. Use the customer's name. Understand your customers' expectations. Anticipate needs. Respond to requests promptly. Get it right the first time. Listen without prejudice. Pick up litter anytime you see any. Follow up and follow through. Make time for excellent service. Remember something small about each customer. Make information easy to find, clearly written and complete. Ask your customers for their input formally and informally.

Common Sense Rule #3

Be nice and practice common courtesies. Always provide a friendly greeting to customers. Always provide a sincere "thanks" as they leave your place of business. Mind your manners and use *thank you, please, yes ma'am, yes sir* and *have a nice day* as if you are sowing seeds of success for your business. In a very real sense, you are.

Common Sense Rule #4

The customer is not always right, but their perception of bad service is a very real thing to them! Don't insult your employees' intelligence by telling them, "The customer is always right." Do create a sensitivity within your organization to the customers' opinions about a certain product or experience. If a customer is unhappy or upset, realize that his reality feels bad to him and he is looking for someone who not only cares, but can help the situation.

Bad service is a bad experience for the customer. Customers are very forgiving to a point, but on occasion, you may discover the proverbial straw that breaks the camel's back with a bad experience. Returning from a week of training in Barbados, I experienced a delay on Thanksgiving Day with BWIA Airlines. Already upset because of a missing baggage situation on the way out, I had been trying for a week to resolve the theft of several items from my baggage when it was returned. This meant making two trips by taxi into town to obtain paperwork. Both times, the person I needed to speak to was "on lunch break" or "not available." I turned in the paperwork at check-in upon departure to be told it would take 12 weeks to reimburse me for the theft.

Back to the delay — knowing this meant I would miss my Miami connection, I knew I would not make a family gathering for the holiday. I boarded in a huff and found I had been assigned a middle seat after requesting an aisle. To add a huge insult to tremendous injury, my meal had a hair in it. When I pointed this out, the flight attendant poked her finger in my food and said, "Where? I don't see any hair." Not only disgusted with her actions, I realized that I had encountered an entire organization that obviously did not care about my bad experience. Did it matter if I was right about the hair? My reality felt horrible and the lack of sensitivity will forever taint my opinion of this airline. Is there anything they can ever do to make it right? Probably not. But had I encountered even one person who truly cared about my experience, it may have made a difference about my perception of their airline.

Common Sense Rule #5

Create a culture for your business and involve your customers in it. Know who you are and what you stand for. How will customers use your products and services? How can you help them gain more enjoyment from your products or services?

Land Rover North Point in Apharetta, GA does an excellent job involving customers in the culture of their products and the experience of off road driving. The dealership showroom is more like a comfy mountain lodge and features a big screen displaying off road adventures. Land Rover gear is available so enthusiasts can look the part. New vehicle owners are invited to a "Fun Day" at a farm to learn the intricacies of driving off road and enjoy a bar-b-que. Land Rover is not just a car, it is a way of life. Always think in terms of the customer's experience at your place of business and beyond to create the kind of relationship that is lasting and loyal.

Opportunity Management

All the common sense in the world won't insure you against the occasional problem and disgruntled customer. There are three simple strategies for handling *opportunities* when they arise.

First, be proactive. Anticipate and avoid problems by being a hands-on manager and teaching your team to look for ways to squelch problems before they take on a life of their own. Reward this kind of behavior frequently and it becomes like a competition to be the shift with the least problems, complaints, returns, etc.

Second, when a situation comes up, and inevitably it will, handle it with confidence. Teach the "no fear" concept to your staff. This means practice of what to say and do in advance by role-playing. It also means getting the message across that employees will not have to fear a negative repercussion when they take an action to correct a problem or make a customer happy. Even if you would have handled it differently, don't punish actions made in good faith — remember you hired people with the right stuff to begin with!

Third step, redirect the negative to a positive outcome for the customer. This will mean individualized solutions and actions based on the customer's needs and expectations. Teach your staff how to ask the questions that will enable them to understand how to customize a solution for the customer. Always follow up and follow through as agreed.

The best service arises from even the smallest opportunities (problems.) Recently on a visit to Wendy's, my husband and I discovered we were seventy-three cents short on our order. After scrounging change purses and under the car seats, we were still short. The young teenager at the counter promptly said, "Don't worry about it, I'll put it in and you can pay me next time you come in!" Her caring service made us less embarrassed and put us in a good mood straight away! This is the kind of care you need to observe and reward in your team. Sometimes little things mean a great deal to the customer.

A much worse problem for me as a customer came in the form of four legs. On a visit to Mauritius to a world class resort, Sun International's St. Geran, I discovered a lizard in my room! Not uncommon in the Indian Ocean, lizards like the cool white walls of the rooms. A young man from Housekeeping quickly came to my rescue. Chasing the lizard outside, my rescuer said in a gentle Indian accent, "The lizard not paid guest, he must sleep outside!" With his efficiency and humor, the employee turned my horror to a great satisfaction and good night's sleep! *No wonder they call St. Geran world class.*

Service Fundamentals

Generating Smiles Daily

Good service is a memorable experience. It grabs the emotions and feelings of the customers and makes them feel happy. Sugar Beach Resort in Mauritius offers a water aerobics class to guests. One hot Sunday morning, I decided to try it out. Conducted entirely in Italian, I was concerned I would not understand the class. It turned out to be the most fun I have ever had exercising! The instructor involved the group of sixty men and women from all over the world in jumping, splashing, singing, floating and generally having a great time in the pool. It was memorable because the water felt cool, the smell of the ocean lingered nearby, the music sounded upbeat and it was a treat to take in the sun-drenched crowd. Our senses were actively engaged. Evidently, the language of fun is universal!

Closer to home, one afternoon I was equally delighted by my hairdresser. She had placed a single black eyed Susan flower in a vase on the counter in front of the chair. When she dried my hair, the flower spun around and around making me and everyone else laugh! Unexpected, creative and cheap, the black eyed Susan was a great experience.

There are endless ways to generate smiles. The list is only limited to the imagination and innovation of you and your team. When you need a little inspiration to get you started, check this list of tried and true SmileMakers[sm]:

Connect with Your Customer

Give customers smile stickers to "reward" excellent service. Provide employees treats to "reward" customers. Take advantage of delays or transfers to get to know customers. Ask customers "How can I make you smile?" Pass along an article you know would be of interest to a particular customer. Encourage staff to build professional relationships with customers. Avoid canned or scripted service. Avoid form letters. Remember food and drink preferences and ask if customer would like the same again. Say "welcome back" upon return visits. Treat customers as the reason for work instead of an interruption to work. Involve back of house staff in programs such as landscape department giving a nature tour or the chef teaching cooking lessons.

Nice Touches

Put fresh flowers in public restrooms. Clean windshields of cars in the parking lot. Leave a scented thank you for valet parked cars. Place magazines or books based on customers interests in waiting areas or guest room. Make tissue paper flowers to top Kleenex dispensers. Use oversized quality amenities in rest rooms. Keep in touch with postcards. Have live operators answer the phone instead of voice mail. Provide umbrella assists on rainy days. Decorate for the holidays. Sponsor community groups to entertain during the holidays. Partner with a local museum to display art in public areas. Provide a walking map of the area as a courtesy. Send a "thank you for your business" note. Use lots of plants in colorful pots for a "homey" feel.

Refresh and Revive

Offer fresh pineapple after sports activities. Provide a cold (or warm) towel upon arrival for freshening up. Supply scented bubble bath in the room. Offer a welcome drink appropriate to your climate. Use energizing lavender or sunflower scented candles in restrooms. Offer neck massage during wait-in-line time. Spritz cool water on hot customers. Put out a lemonade stand during coffee breaks (charge ten cents a cup and donate to charity.) Offer tea in the afternoons. Provide yoga classes. Sell energy snacks in the gym. Set up amenities in rest rooms with powder, deodorant and mouthwash. Offer cinnamon flavored coffee in the morning. Provide personal head sets for books on tape. Use background music that is soothing. Hand out peppermint foot lotion to weary customers. Demonstrate tension relieving stretches every afternoon. Set out dishes of chocolate kisses. Have cool water available anywhere customers may need a drink.

Fun and Games

Perform magic tricks. Make origami. Do a sensory nature walk involving sight, sound, taste, touch and smell. Use fun drink presentations and props. Give a toy or coloring book for business customers to take home to their kids. Use magnetic words on a board to advertise specials or impart information. Put board games and puzzles out. Use small games in restaurants to play while waiting for order. Let employees do a line dance with customers once a week. Set up a customer complaint booth and use invisible ink pens. Create a treasure hunt for discovering your business. Have theme days during which employees dress up or wear hats to celebrate obscure holidays (National Peanut Butter Day.) Start traditions (like the Peabody Duck walk) which are unique to your business. Give out free Alka Seltzer and aspirin packs on New Year's Day. Let local craftsmen exhibit their skills. Float rubber duckies in ponds or pools. Give out silly prizes for things like "best dressed customer." Hold trivia contests if people must wait in long lines. Teach fancy napkin folding.

Blow Them Away

Sing a lullaby to sooth a crying baby. Put stamped postcards on the breakfast table for customers to send home. Acknowledge birthdays or anniversaries. Sneak a little something extra into every purchase or package like a bedtime story or fancy bookmark. Set out cookies and milk with customer names written on the cookies. Spell out children's name in alphabet sponges or magnetic letters in a kids corner. Send a birthday card signed by all staff. Don't charge for local telephone calls. Take Polaroid pictures of customers having fun and give them away in a souvenir logo frame. Serve "smiley face" pancakes. Return lost items before customer discovers they are missing. Notice customers' dissatisfaction before they complain and offer solutions. Go above and beyond the expected. Step outside the definition of your job description every now and again. Call customers and ask when they will be back.

Summary

Use this quick checklist of simple solutions and common sense strategies to create a business focused on the customer.

- ✓ Hire employees who care
- ✓ Manage barriers to service, not people
- ✓ Involve the whole team in service solutions
- ✓ Put employees in positions that highlight their strengths
- ✓ Service unto customers as they wish
- ✓ Mind your manners
- ✓ Never fail to provide a friendly greeting
- ✓ Never fail to provide a sincere thank you
- ✓ Find ways to say *yes,* not excuses for saying no
- ✓ Delight customers with unexpected experiences
- ✓ Encourage fun and play at work
- ✓ Smile yourself!

Being a SmileMaker^{sm} is the most important part of your job. It keeps the focus on the customer in a way that makes work fun for your team. It brings tremendous rewards personally and for your business. You have the power to not only create wonderful experiences for your customer, but for yourself and your staff.

There will be times when you can't put a smile on everybody's face. But out of every problem there is an opportunity to make a smile. Everyone must share a positive attitude about service. Together you can create the experiences that will bring smiles to your customers. The result — pleasant memories that keep them coming back for more!

Bio — Meg McLeroy Croot

Meg Croot is the founder and President of Creative Recommendations, Inc., and is an internationally known consultant, facilitator and resource to hospitality and leisure industries. She is an innovator in helping employees at all levels incorporate creativity into their service interactions and day-to-day experiences. Strategic and a dynamic team facilitator, Meg is committed to teaching individuals and corporations the benefits of adding fun to the daily grind at work and home. Creative Recommendations, Inc. clients include Texas Restaurant Association, Wyndham Hotels, Sun International Hotels, Atlantis Resort and Casino, Boca Raton Resort and Club, The Family Channel and Department of Education.

Contact Info:
Meg McLeroy Croot
Creative Recommendations, Inc.
1310 Land O' Lakes Drive
Roswell, GA 30075
Phone: 770-645-2862
Fax: 770-645-2869
E-mail: mcroot99@aol.com
Web site: www.creative-rec.com

Chapter 5

Mastering the Three Challenges of Customer Service

JERRY L. FRITZ

Meeting the Challenges

Walk into a Nordstrom's department store, track a Federal Express pickup, or talk to a Lands'End catalog phone representative and you will experience world-class customer service. These benchmark companies are recognized throughout the country and overseas as leaders in delivering superior value to their customers. How did these companies gain this coveted status? In a market as crowded as direct marketing, how did Lands' End grow in fifteen years to surpass firms that had been in the business for over fifty years? The answer is that each of these companies adheres to a strict ethic of customer service that permeates the entire organization — throughout every department, function and person.

Is world-class customer service reserved for only the very large company? Not at all. Can your company join the ranks of Federal Express or S. C. Johnson in the eyes of your customers? Absolutely. Only, however, IF you accept the challenge of making customer service the focus of your organization.

Committing to providing superior customer service means being willing to accept the challenges which you must master to attain your goal. These three challenges are outlined in the following graphic.

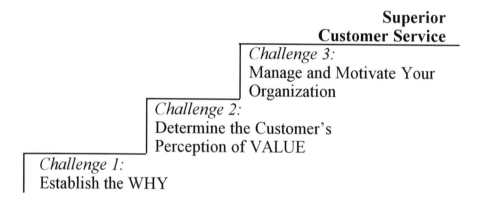

Superior Customer Service

Challenge 3:
Manage and Motivate Your Organization

Challenge 2:
Determine the Customer's Perception of VALUE

Challenge 1:
Establish the WHY

Challenge 1: Establish the *Why*

Do you and your employees know how to take good care of your customers? And if you do, how do you move onto the next level? How do you take your customer service from being good to world class?

Simply knowing how to take *good* care of customers is not adequate for today's business world. If you are preparing to move into the 21st Century, you will need to look for ways to move your level of customer service to the *next* level. Knowing "we *should* do it," just won't get it done. We must establish a "compelling reason *Why*." Just to be able to compete in today's competitive environment, you must provide superior customer service.

Your Competitive Edge

All products and services can and will be duplicated by your competitors. Your customers are very aware of their options and they actually think they can go elsewhere and purchase the same product/service. So, that means you have no competitive advantage when it comes to product or price. Your customer service, however, can be your competitive edge. The unique mix of professional employees, supported by an infrastructure which has set customer service standards at all levels, is the key to success in this highly competitive environment. If you can master the challenge of increasing the level of awareness among all employees as to the vital importance of customer service, you have gained a very important foothold in the climb to the top of your market.

Who is Responsible?

Who is responsible for providing superior customer service? Every employee in your company. Every individual in the business who is directly or indirectly involved in providing a product or service to the customer must be committed to providing outstanding service.

Sometimes it is difficult to get everyone in the organization fired up about participating in the attitude that *everyone* is responsible for customer service. For some people, they need a motivation or a reason *Why* they should 'buy into an idea' such as customer service. Often this lack of motivation and interest on the part of company personnel stems from a lack of awareness. They need a compelling reason WHY customer service is critical to the business. So, what is that compelling reason *Why*? The following exercise will provide you with proof that you can use to establish the *Why*.

Mastering Challenge 1

If you are looking for one idea to create a compelling reason *Why* the customer is so important to your business, determine the exact dollar figure for a single customer. If you were to write a check for the worth of one of your customers, what dollar amount would that be? Impossible task? Absolutely not! There is power in knowing the specific dollar value of a happy, repeat customer who brags about your business to friends and associates.

Take the following restaurant example as an illustration of how a dollar value can be placed on one of your customers. Then note how the dollar value of that one customer can impact your business further by indirect or word-of-mouth advertising. Once you've read down through the example and corresponding formulas, please use the "Your Business" column to calculate the worth of a customer in your own organization. I've made some assumptions, very conservatively, which you may want to customize to what you know about your market and customers.

Example: Restaurant		Your Business
Average customer transaction per sale	$25	_____
Number of sales per year	12	_____
Revenue per year (A x B)	$300	_____
Customer Lifetime in Years (Average 5 years)	5	_____
Customer Lifetime Value (C x D)	$1,500	_____
Happy customer tells 5 people on average (E x 5)	$7,500	_____
Revenue Generated from referrals:		
(Assume only 25% purchase from you) (F x .25)	$1,875	_____
Total Value of one Customer (E + G)	$3,375	_____

Additional Benefits

It is quite obvious that one compelling reason why customer service is important can be determined in dollars and cents. In addition to the monetary value of a customer, the following list outlines some additional benefits of putting the customer first.

- Creates goodwill and enhances your reputation
- Reduces instances of "poor quality"
- Increases opportunity to up-and cross-sell
- Raises the rate of customer retention
- Lowers employee turnover
- Increases margins/profit
- Provides a more positive work environment
- Produces an objective and clearly visible performance measure
- Establishes a competitive advantage
- Can be your "point of differentiation"

Summary

You now have some statistics and provable information to establish the reason *why* customer service is so important to your business. It is critical that you increase this level of awareness to *all* employees in your organization. Together, establish a service ethic (a focus on the customer from all departments and people) within your company that will help differentiate your business and create success in your marketplace.

Challenge 2: Determine Your Customer's Perception of *Value*

In today's marketplace, it is an established fact that the majority of customers want *value* when they buy. Naturally, there will be some customers (studies suggest only 3-7%) who buy on price alone, or at least make it one of their most important purchasing factors. The questions that you must ask, when dealing with these price-sensitive buyers, are — "Do I really want to do business with these customers? Am I better off prospecting for customers who look for *value* and not just price? Is this really a smart business decision? If I sell on price, not value, how will that impact my market share, my own employees, my competition?" The answers to these questions can only be answered by you. It is, however, important that you remain focused on the vision, values and goals of your organization regarding how you want to participate in your marketplace.

What is *Value*?

What is value and how is it defined by your customers? Remember, it is not important what you think value is. What does matter is what the *customer perceives* it to be. To be successful in business today you must strive to create more value, both real and perceived, in the minds of your potential customers. The game is simple, create more value, satisfy more customers, gain market share and make more profit. The important fact is this — the value must be in place *before* you can expect business. Each and every employee must know how they contribute to this value. And, there needs to be performance standards in place to ensure every employee makes a consistent contribution.

Customers define value based on a unique set of criteria and its impact on their business. Customers define the value provided from you, the supplier, in the following five components.

1. Quality — The first component of value is the quality of the product or service your organization offers to the customer. Quality is a vital component of value because it is what will bring customers to your door. An appropriate level of quality earns you the right to play in your marketplace.

Customers challenge you to continually make additional improvements, "bells and whistles" to the product or service, so that they can utilize this additional value to be more competitive in their marketplace. They want you to be continually improving your core offering so they can have a greater impact on their marketplace.

A very important criterion of quality which is critical to both your and your customer's success is called "moment of truth." A "moment of truth," as defined by Jan Carlzon of SAS, is any interaction (not transaction ...interaction) that a customer has with your business. When customers engage your organization, they are keeping score. They keep track of the memorable or "WOW" moments as compared to the "so-so" moments as compared to the "that was awful" moments. When the "so-so" and the "awful" moments begin to outnumber the "WOW," you are in trouble and about to lose that customer to the competition. In other words, do your customers experience a positive impression every time they interact with your business? Do all of your employees understand the importance of ensuring that every interaction with a customer must be a positive event? If you want to offer value to your customers, you must be aware of the fact that every contact and interaction you have with your customers is a "moment of truth."

2. Service Support — Service support is your team commitment to customer expectations. It includes all of your business components and departments which support your company's sales promise — guaranteeing that the customer receives exactly what the company committed to supplying. It is the ongoing development of trust through high levels of service support that must be integrated into your business philosophy which therefore allows you to develop long-term relationships with your customers. Examples of service support include your guarantee/warranty, the level of empowerment earned by your customer contact professionals, your customer satisfaction survey process, and the ability to provide immediate service recovery.

3. Delivery — To satisfy or exceed the customer's expectations regarding delivery, your organization must focus on what is called the eight 'rights of delivery.' These rights, as determined by your customers include *right time, right price, right source/destination, right condition, right quantity, right mode, right product,* and *right packaging.* These rights are the part of your business commitment which are most visible to your customers and your customers' customers; simply put — ship the customer what the customer ordered!

4. Customer Contact Professional — It is no secret that customers like doing business with organizations that employ professional and likable salespeople, order entry staff, customer

service representatives, delivery personnel, and others who have direct customer contact. Anyone in your organization who has direct interaction with your customers must have loyalty to the organization and possess the desire to take outstanding care of the customers. How can your customer contact professionals improve on the following? Are they as knowledgeable as they could/ should be? What is their level of honesty and integrity? Do they practice the skills of common courtesy? Are they trained beyond "smile training"? Are your people ready to do the job as expected by your customers? Will they make a contribution to the value as defined by your market?

5. Investment — It must be clear to the customer that they are making an investment in your organization. And, for that investment, your customer contact professionals will provide a return of the appropriate quality, service support and delivery. Ask yourself these questions: Is the cost of your product(s) or service(s) competitive within the marketplace? Do your customers believe that they are getting a return on their investment when they do business with you? Are you selling products or offering systems which solve the customer's problems? If the answers to these questions are "no," then it is time for you to take a closer look at how you are perceived by your customers. Will they invest in you? And, what will be the return?

Top Service Provider Competencies

Since the customer contact professionals are responsible for delivering the value, what standards of performance do we need to establish on which their behavior should be based? Do you ever wonder what the industry leaders in your field do to make themselves successful? Well, it is not a secret. They have established very specific performance standards that are tied to their corporate values and vision. Their number one focus is on customer service and below are the standards they consistently require of their people:

- identify and provide value from the customer's point of view

- establish trust and build customer loyalty

- maintain a high level of energy and motivation

- display teamwork skills

- maintain absolute loyalty to the organization

- perform job duties in a reliable and professional fashion

- assume ownership of and resolve all problems with which they come into contact

- do whatever it takes to meet or exceed expectations

Mastering Challenge 2

All of your employees should complete the following challenge exercise to determine what your organization can do to improve your offering of value to your customers. With all departments and people involved, you will:

1) develop company-wide understanding of the value as contributed by different segments of your organization

2) identify new thoughts how value can be provided

3) validate some of your current beliefs and

4) further define your message of differentiation.

Be honest and forthright in your answers. Are you a unique force in the marketplace, or are you simply another business trying to survive? Identify those areas in which you are strong but also identify where and how you can make improvements. It is from the answers to these questions that your motivation to improve will occur. Remember, most organizations just *talk* about "better quality," "faster service," "quick turn-around time," or "better designs" without actually identifying their unique competitive advantage in specific terms. This exercise will help you clarify specifically what your advantage truly is.

In What *Value* Is Your Customer Investing?

1. What makes your quality unique in the marketplace?
2. What do you have to offer that your competitors do not or cannot provide?
3. What is special about how you conduct business?
4. How or why is your delivery faster?
5. What is it about your service that sets you apart from the competition?
6. Why should anyone buy from you rather than from the other suppliers in the marketplace?

Summary

Use the results of this exercise to focus on the value in which your customers will be investing. Identify those areas in which you can improve and offer more value to your customers and begin working on these TODAY!

You are now ready to proceed to the third challenge as you learn how to manage and motivate others in your organization and drive home the idea that providing superior customer service is everyone's job.

Challenge 3: Manage and Motivate Your Organization

You have successfully completed Challenge 1 and have established the reason WHY customer service plays a vital role in the success of your business. As a result of mastering Challenge 2, you have determined your customer's perception of value and the role it plays in providing superior customer service. You are now ready to accept Challenge 3; managing and motivating others in your organization. It will be critical for your organization that everyone in the company is 'fired up' and 'tuned in' to providing superior customer service. As you already know, customer service is not a one-person job. It takes *everyone's* involvement. Challenge 3 will help you, as a manager, become a better motivator and a better supervisor. Together, you and others in your organization will work as a team in providing value to your customers.

Customer Service is a Philosophy

If you were to ask any benchmark leader, such as Larry's Markets, The Coleman Company or Disney, why they are the best in their industry, they would respond that customer service is not a department, but rather a philosophy of the organization — the way they do business. Period. These companies train every employee in the organization on customer service skills because they know that everyone is a customer of someone, either internally and/or externally. These industry leaders realize something else. They understand that providing superior customer service is not a top-down or bottom-up plan. On the contrary, it means getting *everyone* involved, at all levels of the company.

Improving Service From the Inside Out

Providing superior customer service begins inside your organization and it starts with you. It will be important to ask yourself, as a manager, what you can do to motivate and coach your employees to accept the challenge to exceed customer expectations. Are you fired up when you go to work each day? Are you excited about what you do? Are you willing to take the time to motivate and coach the people in your company to accept the responsibilities for providing superior customer service? Customer service is practiced by each employee in every level of the organization. And it all begins with your managerial support, involvement, and focus.

Internal Customers and Suppliers

Definition of Customer Satisfaction: *Customer satisfaction is the degree of happiness experienced by the customer which is produced within and throughout the organization — among all departments, all functions, and all people.*

The above definition clearly outlines the significance of how customer satisfaction is a responsibility of everyone in the organization. The following diagram further defines the roles of these individuals as you look inside an organization.

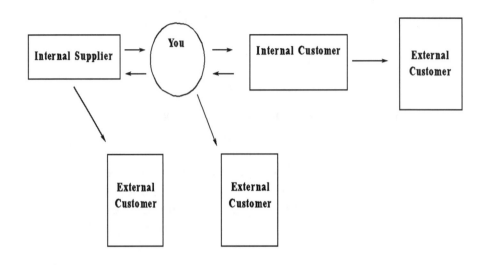

Internal Customers and Suppliers

It is important to understand that every employee in your organization is an internal supplier to other people in the organization. As an example, in a company that manufactures a product, the people who are in packaging or shipping must rely on the individuals who are producing the product. The packaging and shipping departments have a certain number of items to pack and ship each day. They rely on their *internal suppliers* in production to supply them with product to pack and ship. Likewise, the people in production must serve their *internal customers* — the people in shipping. Only when each juncture of internal supplier-customer relationships works together, can the organization as a whole deliver value to the *external* customer.

Mastering Challenge 3

To begin your challenge of managing and motivating people, draw a diagram, similar to the one shown earlier, outlining who the internal customers and suppliers are in your organization. Once your diagram is complete, it will be clear to you who those people are who must communicate and work together as team players in providing superior customer service. Once you have identified the internal customers and suppliers, these team members can then begin to examine how they can work together to better service each other and ultimately the external customer.

The next step in this process, therefore, will be for you to establish team meetings to encourage open communication between team members and departments and establish areas in which improvements should be made. Take five to ten minutes each week to meet with teams and guide them as they begin to understand their roles as internal customers and suppliers of each other.

Use the following exercise to guide you in your team meetings as you motivate and educate employees in the quest for providing superior customer service.

A Team Plan

1. From the diagram you have prepared, make a list of team members and departments (internal customers and suppliers) who must rely on each other's service. Don't forget to include any external suppliers (subcontractors, etc.) that you utilize in your business.
2. Describe the external customer's requirements of your organization. What impact does each team have on ultimate external customer satisfaction?

3. Identify how these team players or this department can improve service to their *internal* customers and *internal* suppliers, which will ultimately affect the external customer.
4. Develop ways to measure internal as well as external customer satisfaction. Remember, you cannot have one without the other!

Summary

You have learned one of the most impactful processes in being able to motivate your customer contact professionals. It will be important to take the information and knowledge that you have learned and challenge yourself to improve your managing and coaching skills. Make a promise to yourself that you will commit to practicing what you have learned. Maintain a positive attitude and hold team meetings to share your enthusiasm with others. And continue to seek ways in which your organization can improve as you prepare to offer superior customer service. Remember, managing and motivating are ongoing challenges!

Staying on Top

Congratulations on mastering the challenges of customer service. Working through these three challenges and evaluating your organization's customer service level has helped you formulate ideas and create plans for improvements. Superior, world-class customer service *is* attainable by your company. Staying on top will, however, require you to be continually driving the Why throughout the organization. Be on the lookout for how you can provide more value to your customers. And, last but surely not least, work hard at the process of *motivating* and *coaching* your customer contact professionals. I invite you to accept the ongoing challenges to make superior customer service a way of life in your organization. The end result — accepting your role as a WORLD-CLASS provider of customer service!

Bio — Jerry L. Fritz

Jerry Fritz is the director of sales and customer service training programs for the Management Institute, the School of Business at the University of Wisconsin-Madison. Prior to joining the Institute in 1990, he had spent 25 years in a variety of customer contact and management positions with North American Van Lines, Inc.; SHADE Paper Company; M.S. Carriers and Roto-Rooter Services Company. Jerry is the author of his forthcoming book entitled <u>19 Skills To WOW Your Customers</u> and is a contributing author to: <u>Best Practices in Customer Service, Celebrate Selling the Consultative-Relationship Way</u> and <u>Breakthrough Customer Service</u>.

Named 1996 marketing educator of the year by Sales & Marketing Executives International (SMEI), Jerry is a speaker at <u>Inc.</u> Magazine conferences on customer service and at the annual meeting of the International Customer Service Association (ICSA). He is also frequently invited to speak to companies as well as provide customized training programs. Jerry is active in several professional associations including: ICSA, SMEI, National Association of Sales Professionals and the National Speakers Association.

Contact Information:

Jerry Fritz
975 University Avenue, Madison, WI 53706-1323
Phone: (608) 262-7331
Toll Free: (800) 292-8964
E-Mail: JLF@mi.bus.wisc.edu or JLF@mi.bus.wisc.edu

Chapter 6

Use the Magical Triad to Pixie Dust Your Organization

JO SPURRIER

I remember when I was preparing to start my career with The Disney Co. and trying to explain to my grandmother just what it was I would be doing at Walt Disney World. I think behind her questions was her fear that her granddaughter, after the time and expense of college, was moving south to be Mickey Mouse! After multiple attempts to explain my future job responsibilities, it dawned on me to "keep it simple" so I merely replied, "I am going to be a 'Pixie-Duster!'" This simple phrase said it all, and in an instant the smile in her eyes told me she understood.

Organizations of all shapes and sizes in all industries are looking for that "special something" that will set them apart from the herd of companies waving the same Customer

Service banner. What sets your organization apart? What is your Pixie Dust? Do you verbalize your service promise… even write it down? Or do you guarantee it? What would it take to go beyond saying it, writing it, or guaranteeing it… but to have your people actually "living it?" What if every person on your staff or team was able to internalize your Service Philosophy so fully, so personally, that it simply is… the way you do business?

I bet right about now, you are thinking that sounds like Fantasy Land! Relax; my feet are firmly set in reality. It is not only possible to achieve a "Living Service Philosophy" but fun and engaging to create it with your staff. OK, sit up and take notice… I said "with your staff." High participation is a direct link to high return on your investment. This is an investment in time and creativity — expensive commodities, but well worth it if you are serious about creating significant change.

The Magical Triad

There are three main levels of customer service we are about to explore. The first level is Creating the Magic. It is at this level that we will identify our Living Service Philosophy (referred to as LSP) which consists of your Service Culture, Theme and Standards. Moving to the second level, we will examine Sharing the Magic. Once you have developed your LSP, how do you spread the word to your entire organization? Lastly, we will discover how to Maintain the Magic. Many organizations are able to attain the "false high" attributed to a new program or company initiative, but more importantly, how do you avoid the "quick fade" that typically follows?

Create the Magic

When I read or hear the name Disney, I am instantly transported back to Missouri on a cold Sunday night. My sister and I would climb up on the couch with our bowls of ice cream (eating in the living room versus the kitchen… big night!) as we turn on our television. Even though it was an old black and white set, I can still picture the vivid colors I saw as Tinkerbell pause in flight to wave her wand spreading her pixie dust as the Wonderful World of Disney weekly movie began. When you read the name Disney, you, too, most likely have an immediate memory or thought associated with it. What words are you thinking of? Happy, fun, movies, Mickey Mouse, children, cartoons, family… The list continues, but is amazingly similar each time I ask that question. When folks share their Disney memories, they are collectively describing Disney's world renowned culture.

Cultures are indeed fragile entities. One of my favorite quotes on the Disney Culture is by John Hench, a Walt Disney Imagineer, exemplifies this perspective:

> Interesting enough for all its success, the Disney theme show is quite a fragile thing. It just takes one contradiction, one out-of-place stimulus to negate a particular moment's experience… tack up a felt tip brown paper sign that says 'Keep Out'… take a host's costume away and put him in blue jeans and a tank top… replace that gay nineties melody with rock numbers… place a touch of artificial turf here… add a surly employee there… it really doesn't take much to upset it all.

This quote causes me to wonder how many times we subconsciously send messages to our customers (and potential customers!) each day. Have you ever been waiting at register while your checker is talking with her friend about what they did last night... or perhaps chatting about the RUDE customer she just checked out? While waiting until Her Highness is ready to ring up your items, your eyes start roving behind the counter. You notice a management note of great importance tacked up for all to read with its yellowed edges ragged and curling. Your eyes take in someone's remains of a snack sitting beside his or her homework. What is your instant impression? What messages about that business' culture have you just received?

It's amazing how we are bombarded with messages about our culture every day. My question remains how many times do we let our culture happen to us versus designing and creating our culture? How many messages, consciously and subconsciously, are you sending your guests or customers about your culture? Organizational Culture is not something any business can afford to take for granted.

In order to create a consistent culture, one that inspires the same descriptors each and every time a potential customer encounters your company, you must first build a strong foundation. A Service Theme must be consistently articulated in order to result in a consistent culture. A consistent message results in a consistent culture.

At this point, I invite you to actively participate. Put down the book and round up pencil and paper. Go! Go now! In order to articulate your Service Theme, we are going to take a snapshot of your organization. Simply answer the question: What do/does you/your company do? Without stating your actual product or service... what do you do? A few innovative workshop responses have been:

- "We get to know you from the inside out!"
- "We help you keep your cool."
- "We are the string for your can."
- "We keep you in the game."
- "We create communities."

(Guess the type of companies these Service Themes belong to? The answers are at the end of this chapter!)

So, what do you do? Have you gotten your answer? There should be no sweaty palms out there; there is no right or wrong response! Once you have established your Service Theme, the next step is to identify your Service Standards. To do so, we merely change the question from What to How you do what you do. What do you value during your daily interactions with your guests? What Service Standards do you communicate in order to uphold your Service Theme?

To jumpstart this process, let's just do a few word associations. Ask yourself, what do you value? Just start jotting down the words that come to mind. Don't worry: if your first thought was, "On a day-to-day basis, we don't value what we say we do!" Relax. This exercise is to raise your awareness and then take it to the next level. So, no matter where you are, our goal remains the same: to move forward.

This revised question asks us to reflect on our values, or our Service Standards. The corporate world refers to them as "Critical Success Factors" or "Objectives." Service Standards being your Service Theme to life. On a daily basis, how do your people know that your front-line folks are supporting your service theme?

The identification of Service Standards serves two important functions. First, it focuses the staff on how they can win. As simple as that sounds, many members of your organization may not be clear about how to win. Usually the pattern is to bounce around in the job for a while trying to figure it out. After getting bumped and bruised, watching others and tuning into the grapevine, they start to figure things out a bit. Just for a moment, think of the incredible power you will generate by showing folks how to win, on day one. The second function is linked to the first. It is the linking of your LSP to behavior and performance. Providing a method of measurement for the softer aspects of business has eluded organizations. Actually, it is not as hard as we have made it out to be. Simply identify specific and measurable Service Standards. For example, be nice to guests is not specific, nor measurable. But, approach and greet each guest by his or her name certainly is. If, in fact, you have specific service standards that everyone is educated and held accountable, and deviation from those standards are not acceptable by anyone, poof! You have a quantifiable way of measurement! This systematic method provides the way of linking performance behavior with your LSP.

Yes, you are correct; we are returning to the basics for a moment. If you were to ask an expert or a master of an industry, thought process, or philosophy, how he or she became an expert, the answer always involves going back to the basics. I would marvel at my Tae Kwan Do teacher, Master Lee. He would spend hours on the simplest, most basic sequences. Catching my eye, he would smile his patient, knowing smile and calmly offer, "Master the basics." I would venture to say in the corporate world it is a common mistake to get caught up and be swept away by the tides of change and innovation, only to discover they've also swept away from the basics. This is no Pixie Dust. This is no magic, but there is magic to be found in reflection of these two fundamental questions. What do you do, and How do you do it?

How does this fit into the "Disney Way?" A goal of The Disney Co. is for its guest to have a seamless experience. When you drive into the parking lot, you should have the same level of service, the same quality experience as when you check into one of their resorts, as when you walk into one of their restaurants, as when you walk into The Magic Kingdom. The values of the Disney organization are not altered, nor sacrificed, no matter what aspect of the company you happen to be engaging.

One of the challenges Disney, like many of your organizations, has to contend with is outside vendors and contracted workers integrated with its cast members. It met this challenge by including in its service agreements a clause contractually requiring the outside party to uphold the same service standards. This vendor responsibility is reinforced by mandatory attendance to The Disney Co.'s Traditions, its legendary orientation experience. Disney's attention to detail results in a seamless experience, one that flows from one to another without lines of service differentiation.

Sharing the Magic

Paramount to the second level of the Magical Triad is the orientation process. Are you aware of the meaning of orient? To look to the east… the orient. To provide guidance or a unified path. Using this definition of orientation, when is orientation? It no longer can be viewed merely as a class or a program. Orientation is an ongoing process of keeping all members of your organization unified and on track. However, you do still need a course or program to initially introduce your company. For example, Disney continually orientates its cast members, but it created a course called Traditions to introduce its new hires to the Disney Way. For the purpose of clarity, when I refer to orientation, I am referencing the actual class or program.

If you have been actively participating, at this point you have a draft of your Living Service Philosophy, which comprises your Service Theme and your Service Standards. Since it is highly unlikely Tinkerbell is going to hire out her services to Pixie Dust your organization, how do you synthesize your LSP into your daily guest interaction? How do you orient your new members?

An organization's first contact with new members is critical to its constantly evolving inner social community. Just like we've been told, first impressions are extremely difficult to change. Therefore, what story are you initially sharing with your new hires? I approach it from this perspective because it truly is just that — a company's first opportunity to tell its "inside" story.

Celebrate, Don't Intimidate:

A shift in your organization's orientation approach to the philosophy of Celebration, not Intimidation will do more for your company morale and sense of community than any holiday turkey or annual picnic ever will. We've all read the studies that shock us with the astronomical monetary comparison of employee retention versus high attrition. This one simple shift in attitude will increase your return on investment tenfold. With this in mind, why aren't more organizations capitalizing on that initial moment they have a captive audience... their introduction to the company... orientation? Sadly, instead this golden opportunity seems to be treated as a necessary evil, or even worse, as an info-dump.

What is the typical orientation comprised of? Forms, forms and forms. Then the infamous orientation video is shown, only to be followed by a dissertation of the company's standard operating procedures manual. I realize this is a dismal, polarized glimpse, but I also contend it holds a few embarrassing truths. In order to Share the Magic, let's look at four elements:

- Content: What story are you telling?
- Facilitation: Who was selected to tell your story, and how were they prepared?
- Participation: Who is required to attend?
- Location: Where is it held, and why was that location selected?

Content:

Do you really have to spend an hour and a half doing the paperwork at orientation? Is there truly a good reason the new member can't fill out the W-4 and other forms at the point of hire? The usual response to that is, "Well if they don't show up for orientation, we've already invested time in their paper process!" Well, let's look at that from a different perspective. Do you think the chances of return are increased if the person has already filled out the paperwork and leave the point of hire as a legitimate member of your community? Hhhmmm something to think about! If you are told by law it must be done at orientation, I would submit it is not law, but instead a company sacred cow: "But, we've always done it that way!"

So, now that we have just created more time to work with, what is it you want to say? Think about it this way: what do you want those new members to go home excited about? What do you want them talking about to their friends and family? What information, in a day that they are likely to forget a lot about, do you want them to remember? A simple foundation consisting of Past — Present — Future will provide a nice format to tell your story.

Facilitation:

Who is your storyteller? When selecting this important individual or team, remain focused on your story. These persons as they stand up in front of your new hires, they are the company. The facilitator's attitudes, morals, standards and philosophies about the company ARE the company to each new member. Who will be able to get your point with the most impact?

Is your theme "we're all in this together," or perhaps "I remember when?" Peer facilitation has its merits, as well as top management or an HR representative. Some companies have structured orientation to include all three at appropriate times. This approach, however, requires coordination and priority from multiple departments. Whatever format you decide upon, take a few moments to match it with the facilitator able to provide the most powerful impression.

Participation:

Typically, who attends orientation? Front-line and maybe middle management. Why do we not extend the same invitation to all levels? When is someone "too high up" and does not need to hear your story? I realize this is a radical idea for some organizational cultures. Yet, what you value and how you conduct business on a day-to-day basis develops your culture. Perhaps the answer to integrating these varying levels of staff is to structure two orientation phases. Everyone attends Phase I and experiences the same first day at their new company. Phase II, is distinctive and specialized to their area of expertise or department.

The mere fact that all, and I mean all, new members attend your orientation sends a very powerful message indeed. A consistent message results in a consistent culture.

Location:

This category usually receives a few chuckles, probably because many of you are dealing with the same frustrations of "Give me a room, any room will do!" The point of location is again to maximize your impact. Adult learners derive 22% of their communication from their surroundings. It is with this fact in mind that we must respect our location. A coat of paint, a few inspirational posters and a tidy room can go a long way if you have limited options for space.

Disney has created a room they call the "Milestones" room. It is just that — a room themed with a series of visual prompts depicting The Disney Co.'s history. As a new hire to the company, just by walking the room's perimeter, one unconsciously absorbs Disney's triumphs, philosophies and goals.

Keeping these four elements in mind as you evaluate your current orientation class will allow you to tell your company's story. Each organization has its own history, present operations and aspirations for the future. Upon joining your community, your company's roots have just become each new hire's corporate history.

Maintaining the Magic

The third level of the Magical Triad deals with one of the most frequently asked questions: "We just held a great training class, and now that everyone is pumped up after this training, how do we keep the excitement alive?"

If, indeed, your quality service initiative is a program or a workshop, you will experience a quick high followed by a quick fade. You are right! But if you have linked your performance standards with your LSP and you are holding people accountable, your Living Service Philosophy becomes a way of life. It is merely the way you do business, not a program, an initiative or a workshop. When your LSP is demonstrated daily, it has become a part of your corporate folklore.

If I ask you to finish the sentences — The legend of... What comes to mind? Sleepy Hollow. You bet. How about — he huffed and he puffed and he... blew the house down. Over the hill and through the woods to... Grandmother's house we go. There was an old woman who lived in a... shoe. Why does each of us know the ending of those sentences? Because, like all pieces of folklore, they have been handed down through the generations sharing with us their lessons of life. Each time they are retold they leave a nugget of knowledge. Your organization also has lessons to hand down to its people. By incorporating the use of folklore in our management strategy, we put another powerful tool in our belt.

Walt Disney was known for his "Management by Wandering Around" philosophy — a slightly different take on the then-popular "Management by Walking Around" strategy. Wandering around lacks the direction and purpose of walking around. It indicates a more casual "where I end up is where I am going" attitude. This is an example of management by folklore, a moment in your organization's past which was built upon and retold to make a point or to reinforce a company value.

Years ago Walt Disney saw the value of folklore: And out of our years of experimenting and experience we learned one basic thing about bringing pleasure and knowledge to people of all ages and conditions which goes to the very roots of public communication. That is this the power of relating facts, as well as fables, in story form.

Who are your company heroes? What stories are you telling? Who are you rewarding, and why? Your answers to these questions will indicate a lot about your present culture. Folklore is a powerful way to transfer information and knowledge. Walt was not only 'wandering' around, he was maximizing each moment of truth he happened upon. Moments of potential tragic turned into magic by not letting them slip by. Each time a moment is transformed, another piece of folklore has been written.

Continually people comment, "Sure, it works for Disney, but will it work at my company?" The answer is without a doubt, yes! Now, with that response befall a few responsibilities. There is no formula for success when implementing another company's winning philosophies. However, a few helpful hints may lessen the bumps on the road to your success. Before you take the plunge and shake up your present status quo, I would invite you to first take an honest assessment of your culture.

- ✓ Are your management and staff capable of adapting to this type of thinking?
- ✓ Do you have the needed systems in place to support your efforts?
- ✓ Resources for the necessary training budget.
- ✓ Capable, willing, and motivated facilitators.
- ✓ Most importantly, the identification of an internal champion to drive the process.

The second hint is to adhere to the rule of Adapt, don't Adopt. Many times the good intentions of a change agent are lost because of the oversight to take time to personalize the program of choice. This disregard fails to take into consideration the personality of your organization and its most valuable resource, your people. By taking the time to shape and mold a program to tailor-fit your world, you are acknowledging the members of your community are already doing quite a bit right. This awareness allows your adaptation of a new culture to be viewed as a natural evolution.

By Creating, Sharing, and Maintaining a clear vision, your organization can experience the power of a Living Service Philosophy. However, like Disney, ultimately the extent of your success will depend upon hard work and attention to detail. These two elements along with a sincere desire to spread your own blend of Pixie Dust will ensure the Disney Way works magic in your world.

P.S. The Service Themes of industries referenced earlier are:
"We get to know you from the inside out!"   MRI Co.
"We help you keep your cool."   Air Conditioning Co.
"We are the string for your can."   Local Phone Co.
"We keep you in the game."   Sports Arena
"We create communities."   Realty Co.

Now, what's yours? I'm always looking for great examples. If you have a catchy Theme and would like to share, I would love to brag about you to others!

Bio — Jo Spurrier

Jo Spurrier is the founder and President of Alliance, Inc., a consulting firm specializing in customized training and workshops designed to move individuals and organizations to the "next level" of competency in today's rapidly changing business world. Her areas of interest include: Teambuilding, Personal Development; Customer Loyalty and Managing Tomorrow's Workforce.

From the corporate ranks of The Disney Company to Experiential Education deep in the forest, her humorous, innovative style provides a dynamic learning environment which challenges all levels of staff to move beyond their perceived boundaries to exceed their goals. Jo's most fundamental belief is when people are engaged in the process and having fun, learning will come naturally!

Jo has a Masters Degree in Organizational Communication and has been working in the field of adult education for the past decade. Jo designed and implemented workshops for a diverse base of client from Fortune 100 Companies to Non-Profit Associations. Clients include Motorola, Barnett Bank, Cleveland Museum of Art, Sabah Development Bank in Malaysia, Thompson Medical Center in Singapore, Enterprise Rent-A-Car, and Inc. Magazine Conferences.

Contact Information:
Jo Spurrier
Alliance, Inc.
417 NE 15th Avenue, Ft. Lauderdale, FL 33301.
Phone: 954-527-0140
E-mail: ALLIANCEjo@aol.com

Chapter 7

Build Your Customer Base and Career Quickly with Five S.M.A.R.T. Ideas for Placing Your Customers at the Center of the Universe

DOUG SMART, CSP

The last time you bought from a flower shop, did you choose it because of:

a. convenience?

b. fair prices?

c. excellent work?

d. or, you like the owners so much you wanted them to have your money?

As a business trainer, the only time I've heard someone in the audience pick "d" was because the owners were her parents. You chose to do business with your florist for a reason that centered on *your* needs not on the *owners'* needs. In that small business decision you maneuvered yourself into the place at *the center of the universe* — because the focus of the business transaction was on *your* needs and wants. I bet that if the florist advertised their location as inconvenient because the rent was cheap, their prices too high because they didn't have the will power to control costs and their work crummy because sticking flowers in a jar of water is no big deal, you wouldn't voluntarily patronize it, because *your* needs wouldn't be met. In other words, if the business focused on their needs, not yours, and plopped themselves instead of you in the center of the universe, you'd be turned-off as a customer. And turned-off customers buy less — if at all; they are not repeat customers if the competition provides better alternatives (and failure to win repeat customers is a death sentence for any business); and they badmouth the place, driving away potential business. Here's a simple tenant for success: There is only room for one person at a time in the center of the universe — and the choices are the service provider or the customer. When the service provider is in the center position, the business loses. When the customer is in the center, the business has a chance of winning. OK, so this sounds like a no-brainer — what's the point?

Frequently, sloppy customer service that drives you and me away is nothing more than the service provider focusing on himself and not on you or me. For example, you are frantically looking for your purse, and the pizza delivery guy hollers through your screen door, "C'mon lady! I haven't got all night!" Intellectually you know his words are true, but emotionally you feel antagonized because he focused on *his* plight and not *your* frustration. If he had said in a reassuring tone, "I know you're trying hard to find it fast. Thanks. That'll help me make more deliveries tonight," you'd probably double the size of the tip to compensate him. All the savvy delivery person did in the second example was to put *you* instead of *himself* in the center of the universe. What a difference in positive feelings that provokes in the customer! And customers love to do business when and where they feel good.

Here's another example that is common: A new business installs a changeable letter sign that flashes, "You've tried the rest now try the best!" — a cute rhyme, but who's at the center of the universe? The business, not the customer! Why? The business is pounding its chest, proclaiming it's wonderful. But who cares? We expect every business to have high business self-esteem. If we thought they didn't believe in themselves, we wouldn't want to patronize them anyhow!

Through the years I've had coworkers with the attitude, "Look, I just want the customer to buy something so I can make my sale and get my commission. I don't want a relationship and I don't care if they are at the center of the universe — I just want my money." Let me ask you, even through the smiles and making nice-nice, can't you spot a phony who's pretending to care about you in order to hurry you up to buy something? Your radar knows the salesperson is putting *himself* — not you — at the center of the universe. When you can't contentedly occupy the center, you feel uncomfortable and probably unappreciated, and you don't feel any particular connection to returning there or recommending that business to others. The salesperson loses in the long run.

When you are the customer service provider, what's in it for you when you concentrate on placing your customer in the center of the universe? You win!

- Loyal customers come back, so you make easier sales.
- Repeat customers spend more money so you're better rewarded financially.
- You get referral business and they are sold on you before meeting you.
- Your income is steadier and more predictable.
- Your value in business is evident, appreciated, and compensated.
- Success draws success so more business appears.
- Your career gets red-hot.
- Opportunities develop to take your talents in fresh directions.
- You rise faster to the top of your profession.
- People seek your advice — you become a guru.

Zig Zigler, in <u>See you at the Top</u>, has written that if you help enough other people get what they want the world will give you what you want. How do you help lots of people get what they want? Easy. As you have business dealings with them, place each of your customers in the center of the universe when you are working with them. Get smart.

Five S. M. A. R. T. Ways to Place Your Customers at the Center of the Universe

Start by Asking, Listening and Taking Notes

Why wait for feedback to drift to you? It's comforting to think *no news is good news*, but in a hyper-competitive world it might be that no news means you are in an information coma. A quote from Sam Walton, founder of Wal-Mart, currently the highest sales retailer on earth, is painted in large letters on a wall in the world headquarters, "The key to success is to get into the store and listen to what the associates have to say. It's terribly important for everyone to get involved. Our best ideas come from clerks and stock boys." If "Mr. Sam," as he's lovingly referred to by Wal-Mart associates, knew to listen to his front-line people for real-world feedback, doesn't it make sense that you and I should "get into the store" and listen to what the decision makers — our customers — have to say? When's the last time you personally asked your customers what they like about shopping with you and your competitors? Have you asked them what they dislike about your competitors — and you? If you have the intestinal fortitude, can you ask them how they feel about doing business *with you as a person?*

More question-asking and listening not only positions the customer at the center, it also makes sales. For example: We decided we should have a great stereo at home, and I knew it would be expensive. I'll confess, there are no audiophiles in our house. Being a visual person, I figured the fastest way to get an education was to make a few early evening explorations to stores that sold stereo equipment and to discover what features were available at the different price levels. Then, a week later, I'd go back to buy one. At the first store, the two salespeople standing idly near the door looked in the direction of a pimply faced young man and indiscreetly signaled, "You're up." He approached us awkwardly, so I easily brushed him aside with a friendly, "We're just looking today." He asked what we were looking for and pointed us toward stereos. It was fun wandering through a sound system playground — reading tags, pressing little buttons, comparing values. Ten minutes later he approached us again and started a conversation. He asked about the system we had currently and what was good and bad about it. He wanted to know what type of music we enjoyed. He asked what room the new stereo would be in and how big it was. While he was asking these questions in a friendly, nonthreatening, conversational way, he started jotting notes about our wants on a yellow pad. After a couple of questions about price, we made it clear cost would definitely be a determining factor, and he continued asking questions about our needs. He made recommendations but mostly asked more questions and made notes of what we said. It was as if we had asked the nice, knowledgeable teenager next door for advice before we flung ourselves into the scary world of stereos. All the while he was capturing our thoughts on his yellow pad. I must admit, having the attention focused on us versus having the attention centered around selling the stuff on the shelf felt refreshing and reassuring. He was knowledgeable about sound systems, and I felt safe to confide my biggest stereo fears to this boy-stranger. I felt he understood. Feeding back to me my concerns and frequently my very words, he guided us through the stereo department like a loving safari guide who had lived his whole life in that treacherous, unfathomable jungle. The upshot of this retail drama — we left an hour later with a new stereo system.

As a follow-up note to this story: I have made a lot of money because of that stereo- shopping trip. His style of putting the customer at the center of the universe by asking questions and taking notes felt right. I started doing the same as a real estate agent, and I developed a loyal following of customers who not only bought from me but also referred their friends to me because, as many of them said, I was "the only one who listened." Yellow pads became an important piece of customer service equipment. Three years after the stereo purchase, the trade association I belonged to awarded me *life membership* in the Million Dollar Club for consistent outstanding sales volume, and I credit much of that success to asking questions and taking notes.

Here's a second follow-up note: The stereo salesman and I have stayed in touch. Fortunately for him, he enjoyed a healthy commission scale that rewarded his skills. Within a year he bought investment real estate through me, introduced me to his fiancee, and treated himself to a car with the shiniest, blackest paint job I'd ever seen (even though I suspect it was a used one); it was a Porsche!

The payoff for placing the customer at the center of the universe is a strong one, and a simple way to do it is to ask questions and take notes.

I'm a professional speaker and I own a keynote and training company. My first contact with a potential client is usually by phone. In our preliminary conversation I immediately start asking questions to find out if I am right for him or her — and I tell the caller I'm taking notes on a yellow pad. This helps him or her feel positioned at the center of the universe, and it helps me later know how to develop my talk. I try not to ask "yes or no" questions because I want to learn from the conversation where their *heads and hearts are* on the issues. Here are the main questions that work for my clients and me (Note: This is accomplished conversationally and not as a grilling! As the conversation progresses, some of these I decide to save for later, and many are answered before I get to ask them):

What is the purpose of your meeting? What is the theme? What are the dates? Which topic of mine are you interested in? Why this topic at this time? If you hire me, what outcomes do you want? What might currently get in the way of your people having their best year yet? What changes is your business experiencing? How well are people adapting? What is something your team has done this year that you're particularly proud of? Who is your competition? In what areas are you better than your competition? Where is the competition gaining on you? What keeps you awake at night? If you were giving a talk on _____, what are three points you would want the attendees to be sure to remember long after the talk? Have you worked with a professional speaker before? What did you particularly like about the last speaker you hired? What do you wish he/she had done better? What's your budget? Who will make the final decision on a speaker? When?

The conversation usually lasts 10 to 20 minutes, and I gather several pages of notes. My clients teach me what their challenges are. This gives me insight on how I can help their situation. Also, by revealing what they liked and didn't like about my speaking peers, they signal what I need to do to make them happy — no guesswork on my part. And the potential client, comfortable at the center of the universe, feels heard and appreciates that he or she is working with someone who is positioning himself to offer sizzling customer service.

I just gave you examples of questions that work when selling an intangible, like a keynote. But what kind of questions can you ask if you are selling a tangible product, like, say, men's suits? How about: Do you need the suit for a special occasion? How soon? Where else will you wear it? What business are you in? What brands have you found fit most comfortably? What brands don't fit? What is your favorite color? Any colors you dislike? How do you feel about the new synthetic fabrics? Do you wear your jacket buttoned or open? Do you favor white, pastel, or dark shirts? What type of statement do you like to make when you enter a room — quiet dignity, head-turning, or somewhere in-between? What price would you like to stay under? What do you think of this shirt, tie and belt combination with this suit?

Customers expect professionals to ask questions. Doctors ask questions and as patients we give answers. In fact, we'd distrust the professionalism of a doctor who didn't ask questions. Smart customer service people are professionals who ask questions. If you were the customer, and the above questions were asked in a caring, conversational tone of voice and in an unobtrusive manner, would you feel you were working with someone better than average? Would you rate that person as someone who is going places in that business? You bet!

Your Turn

Placing Your Customers in the Center of the Universe

List five questions you can ask your customers within moments of meeting so you can find their wants and needs.

1. _____

2. _____

3. _____

4. _____

5. _____

Maintain the Proper Perspective: Give in When it Makes Sense

Today is blistering hot, and after two days of being on the fritz, our central air conditioning is running again. My wife, Gayle, our two children and I have suffered two fitful, sticky, sleepless nights — plus, we have weekend house guests arriving tonight! Presently, we are a family of grumpy bears!

As Gayle and I have pieced together the story of our predicament, it is clear to us the air conditioning worked as good as new after we had the unit serviced a couple of weeks ago. The trouble actually started four days ago when we hired "Mr. Sparky, America's Favorite Electrician" to replace a bathroom circuit breaker that had gone kaput. After he left, the bathroom outlets worked fine, but the air conditioning and the lights in the foyer didn't. We called immediately, and the electrician returned within an hour. He said, "I got the lights back on but I can't figure out why the air conditioning doesn't run. It must be a coincidence. I guess you should call your AC company back. Maybe they can figure it out." Two days later the air-conditioning technician's test indicated the equipment was fine, but no electricity was getting to the unit. After simply jiggling the circuit breaker box in the basement, it started working. He didn't know why and didn't understand what he did that made it work. Fine. Concerned about the fire hazard of wires so loose they can be jiggled, Gayle called the owner of "Mr. Sparky" and asked that he send a senior electrician to check us out — and also that his company pay the $22 air-conditioning service call. He agreed to have it looked into. In the meantime the air conditioning quit on us again.

Two days later the owner himself arrived to check out the situation. He determined the challenge was an aging, faulty circuit breaker, which he replaced, and then he presented us with a bill. Gayle, believing in fairness and in the old wisdom, "You don't ask, you don't get," clearly and confidently stated we would pay for material but not for labor since this should have been spotted on the first visit, and that we should pay only the wholesale cost of the material to compensate for mental anguish — plus we would deduct the $22 cost of the air conditioning contractor's bill. "Mr. Sparky" started to protest and then smiled. "OK, that'll be fine," he said and genuinely added, "I want you to be happy." Gayle felt the situation was resolved fairly and to her satisfaction. We figure he knew he could have left with $75 more, but he probably realized there are 1,000 homes in our development, and as in most Atlanta neighborhoods, neighbors love to express opinions about who is and isn't good to work on our homes. Will we call him again? Yes, without hesitation. Will we recommend him to neighbors and family? Yes, easily, because we believe the work is good and his attitude is customer focused.

Maintaining the proper perspective helps keep the customer at the center of the universe. That's smart service. *The customer's always right* may be a tired old saying, but the reality of today's marketplace is it costs much less in the long run to keep a current customer than to get a new one. A top-notch motivational speaker, Mike Marino, who owned a successful retail business for over 20 years, jokingly says, "You can be right, or you can be happy!" It pays to give in when it makes sense.

Your Turn

Placing Your Customers in the Center of the Universe

List five past situations in which you could have "given in" without giving the store away and probably would have gained a loyal customer.

1. _____
2. _____
3. _____
4. _____
5. _____

Always Create an Environment That Places the Customer in the Center of the Universe

Another easy way to offer sizzling customer service is to create an environment in which the customer feels comfortable doing business with you. I was in a New Orleans department store during that throw away week between Christmas and New Year's, enjoying the holiday music wafting about and the tranquil rest of a descending escalator ride, when I heard an upset customer shouting at a salesclerk. In the fur department at the foot of the escalator, a nicely dressed but hostile woman with a bulky fur coat draped over one arm was giving an employee a piece of her mind — and some of the language was brutal. Sensing an opportunity to do some customer service field research, I decided to shop in the fur department.

"You stupid people never get anything right! You ruined my coat! I want you to take this back, and I want my money now!" she bellowed. The saleswoman, also well groomed, maintained her composure. The look of concern on her face, the slight tilt of her head and almost imperceptible nodding indicated she was registering everything. She did not speak words, but her face asked "What? What happened? Why are you doing this?" The customer was practically ranting. The saleswoman took a half step backward. The customer took a half step forward. The saleswoman took another small step backward and the customer closed the distance. She did it again and the customer followed. A couple more steps behind her was a pretty French-style desk with a commanding leather chair behind it and two small, fancy, French-style chairs in front. She sat in one of the fancy chairs, and the customer lowered herself into the other. All this time the saleswoman was virtually silent, but her customer service mastery was evident to me.

The nasty customer was led to the desk and chair area — the proper place for conducting business properly. When the customer sat down, she lowered her tone of voice, too. When the voice lowered, the choice of ugly words dropped with it. Taking a chair beside the customer signaled, "I'm on your side," which helped to further defuse the moment. Apparently sensing it was now time to do business, she started asking questions. She let the talking customer take the center of the universe, this time with civility.

I eavesdropped — as much as I could! In response to questions the customer spoke rationally. Here are the facts as

I overheard them: She had long dreamed of owning a big mink coat and finally bought one for herself as a holiday gift. She was excited until it arrived and a crushing disappointment overwhelmed her — one of the three initials in the embroidered monogram was wrong. Her coat was "ruined," even though she clearly gave the correct initials to another (not present) salesperson.

I knew that when the *other salesperson* was brought up the saleswoman had an easy opportunity to extricate herself from this encounter — but she chose to stay on course. She could have pitched blame on the *other salesperson* ("Yes, we've had problems with her before") or on the customer herself ("Let's just get the order book out right now and see what initials you gave us!"). Instead, she chose the high road. She apologized that an unfortunate mistake had occurred. She offered to have the monogramming redone, but the customer steadfastly refused that option because "patching it" would make it feel like second-hand goods to her. Like a friend, the saleswoman continued asking questions along the lines of, "What made you fall in love with this fabulous coat? Do you agree it was a good value? What will it take to make you absolutely happy with this coat of a lifetime?" The customer dropped her defensive posture. She really wanted the coat! And I'm sure the saleswoman was savvy enough to understand that the customer was more in need of an emotional outlet than of having her money refunded. The result of this talk: The customer agreed to keep the mink if the store replaced the entire silk lining and embroidered a new monogram. They shook hands. As I see it, the customer service skill of the saleswoman created a win/win/win/win: The calmed customer made a rational decision to keep her coat; the store kept the income from a very high ticket sale; the *other salesperson* collected a healthy commission; and the smart saleswoman further enhanced her value in business by turning a potential disaster into a stunning victory.

You and your customers win when you create an environment customers want to be in. Think about when you are the customer: Do you prefer to do business in places that help you feel calm and receptive or in those that aggravate you so much you feel perpetually defensive? Do you prefer to spend your money in businesses that adjust to your feelings or in those that make you contort to their rules?

Your Turn

Placing Your Customers in the Center of the Universe

List five things you can do to create a more customer friendly atmosphere.

1. _____

2. _____

3. _____

4. _____

5. _____

Remember — Don't Assume Customers Know What You're Talking About

Sometimes customers do strange things because they don't understand what is said to them. *The Wall Street Journal* relates the following examples: Offering computer know-how via the telephone, an AST Technical Support staffer asked a customer to send a copy of her defective diskettes, and a short time later an envelope arrived with *photocopies* of the diskettes. Compaq Computer is discussing dropping the command "Press Any Key" and replacing it with "Press Return Key" to stem the barrage of calls for help finding the "Any" key.

In the real estate business, just like in your business, we flung around "shop talk" words and phrases (like *equity, debt-to-earnings-ratios,* and *private mortgage insurance*) as though everyone knew what they meant. The customer is not in the center of the universe if he or she cannot understand your language. It's smart to make communication easy for both the customers and you. Be certain you can be understood.

Your Turn

Placing Your Customers in the Center of the Universe

List five technical terms you use that have customers asking "what did you say?" Next to them list 5 phrases you can use instead.

1. _____

2. _____

3. _____

4. _____

5. _____

Try to Give Service They'll Talk about for Years to Come

There is an American proverb: "Everybody loves a winner." Delta Air Lines is fortunate to have a winner, flight attendant Michael McGhee, aboard as he embodies *put the customer at the center of the universe* customer service. I like to write while on the plane, and on a recent trans-America jaunt he and I chatted about this chapter. After a little prodding from me, he related the following:

I was working in first class when a pocket of turbulence jolted the aircraft and sloshed red wine onto a passenger's white dress shirt. Instantly, he wiped at it furiously, but the cotton grabbed hold and it [the stain] spread wide. He asked for my help. I had him go into the lav and remove his shirt. In the galley, I poured club soda on the stain to dilute it. This helped some, but it didn't really remove the stain, so I quickly searched my flight bag for something stronger. There's a new product available for lifting stains and it comes in small wet sheets in foil packets that you tear open so you can have one handy when you need it. I always travel with a couple of these in my flight bag; I used one on his shirt and scrubbed until, eventually, the stain did come out. Unfortunately, his shirt was now clean but a damp wrinkled mess. I passed it to him. He was grateful to have the shirt spotless because, he told me, he had an important meeting to attend upon arrival and wouldn't have time to go to a store and buy a new shirt. I knew I could do better than this. So, without hesitation, I reopened my flight bag and over his protestations I insisted he take the clean, pressed shirt that I was going to wear on day two of my trip. I directed him back into the lav to try it on. Luckily it fit and he was back in business. The problem was solved. He thanked me a dozen times.

When he mailed my shirt back to me, he also sent a glowing letter to Delta commending the customer service rendered above and beyond the call of duty. It was really thoughtful of him to write, but I felt happy to have solved the problem for him.

We talked further, and in response to many questions from me, Mr. McGhee divulged he has over 50 letters in his personnel file from passengers who have written Delta to articulate their appreciation for the great job he is doing. He told me,

It's nice when they take the time to write and give me a little pat on the back to say "thank you for a job well done." Each year, when I have a file review, my supervisor remarks at what an achievement that is and how other flight attendants don't come close to acquiring such a level of letters. My supervisor also stated that in this world where everyone is in a rush, people rarely take the time to write. For me, it's just nice to get an affirmation that I'm doing my job well.

Be a winner. Try to give smart service they'll talk about for years to come. Go out of your way to provide outrageously memorable customer service. Why? See if you agree with these three reasons. You will delight the customers enough to encourage their repeat business. You will build a career on as solid a foundation as possible. (Quick test: If you were Mr. McGhee's supervisor and the order came down to reduce the number of flight attendants, do you think you would release one of your star performers to the competition?) You will fall in love with your job — again.

Your Turn

Placing Your Customers in the Center of the Universe

List five things you have done that rate as *above and beyond*-type customer service they'll talk about for years to come. If you can't think of five in the past, list five in the future that you'll try so you build a reputation for sizzling customer service.

1. _____
2. _____
3. _____
4. _____
5. _____

Build your customer base and your career quickly by placing your customers at the center of the universe. This smart approach will help you avoid the common, business-eroding trap of sloppy customer service that drives them away because the service provider focuses on himself and not on the customer. A simple-to-remember and easy-to-apply approach is to get **S. M. A. R. T.**:

Start by asking, listening, and taking notes.
Maintain the proper perspective; give in when it makes sense.

Always create an environment that places the customer in the
    center of the universe.

Remember — don't assume customers know what you're
    talking about.

Try to give service they'll talk about for years to come.

Bio — Doug Smart, CSP

Call Doug Smart, CSP, to get participants laughing, learning, and leading. Doug is an author, radio personality, keynoter, and trainer who has spoken at over 1,000 conventions, conferences, seminars, sales kickoffs, and management retreats. He works with leaders who want to make this their best year yet! Doug's *"Smart Ideas Series"* boosts resiliency, productivity, leadership, and creativity. His diverse client list includes AT&T, Columbia HCA, IBM, Mitshubishi Motor Sales, Southern Methodist University, Kansas State Government, and U.S. Department of Education.

Doug is the author/co-author of: *TimeSmart: How Real People Really Get Things Done at Work, TimeSmart: How Real People Really Get Things Done at Home, Reach for the Stars, FUNdamentals of Outstanding Dental Teams,* and *Where There's Change There's Opportunity!*

Contact Information:

Doug Smart
Doug Smart Seminars
P.O. Box 768024 Roswell, GA 30076
Phone: (770) 587-9784
Fax: (770) 587-1050
E-mail: DougSmart.Seminars@att.net

Please E-mail Doug's office to request a free subscription to "SMART IDEAS for Leaders" E-Newsletter.

Chapter 8

PATTY KITCHING

The Secret Ingredients for Super Customer Service

"Patty, we need customer service training." During the sixteen years I have been conducting training seminars, I have heard this statement many times, and it always makes me cautious. The clients making the request range from high-tech companies to health-care corporations, retail stores to the automotive industry. They know that keeping customers happy is the key to success. That much is obvious. And sometimes customer service training is just what is needed. But not always. In fact, it has been my experience that the obvious problem is rarely the real problem.

What do I mean? Surely, if we hire the right people and train them on good customer service skills, the result will be satisfied customers. Won't the ratings on the customer satisfaction survey climb, the complaints decrease and profitability soar? That is what clients want to hear. Just run a few classes, teach those customer contact people to be pleasant at all times, smile, go the extra mile and deal with those difficult customers, and we'll have this problem solved.

I wish! It would certainly make my job easier. But it rarely works that way, because the real problem is hidden. The real problem is below the surface. The real problem isn't the customer contact people at all. The real problem is management.

Why would I suggest, even insist, that poor management, inadequate supervisors and lack of support from leaders is the real culprit, the root cause of mediocre to lousy service? Let me explain.

Let's consider a scenario far removed from the world of business. Let's imagine for just a moment that we have a group of underprivileged children, age five, who are about to enter public school for the first time. Because these children have been in home situations where they have not been exposed to some basic socialization skills, they are missing some essential behaviors and attitudes required for success in school. In fact, they have never even been taught to say "please" and "thank you" — important basics!

The well-meaning decision makers decide to solve this problem by sending the five-year-olds to a seminar. After all, a week in class should do the trick. The class will be fun and informative. The instructor will explain how important it is to say "please" and "thank you." The children will share how it makes them feel to be treated politely. There will be lots of role playing in which they get to practice their new skill, saying "please" and "thank you." Then, after emphasizing how important it is for them to put their new-found skills to use, they'll be sent back home.

How long will the new behavior last? Anyone who has ever worked with children can tell you: not long, maybe a few days; with the brightest and most motivated, maybe a few weeks. It's easy to see that the children will fall back into their old behavior patterns in a matter of days. Without a mom who prompts, "What do you say?" without a dad to reward the request prefaced by "please," the child will slip back into old but comfortable ways of interacting. Without daily reinforcement from parents, peers, siblings or teachers, the newly acquired use of "please" and "thank you" will quickly be extinguished.

But we are now talking about adults — professionals attending a seminar on critical skills for success! Surely they will retain and use their new-found skills. They will demonstrate their enlightened and improved attitudes toward customer service. Yes! They will! For a few days. With the brightest and most motivated, maybe for a few weeks. But will it last any longer than that? It can, but only if the essential ingredients are in place.

What are those essential ingredients? Let's explore that question a bit. We tell ourselves that adults are different from children — that you only need to let them know when something is not up to par. But are they really? My sixteen years of experience in training adults was prefaced by seven years of teaching small children. There are obvious differences, but the one common factor for sustaining learning was *practice with praise* — a chance to use the new skill and praise for progress.

Change is difficult. Even if it is a change we elect to make because we believe it to be to our advantage, it is still challenging to let go of old habits and try something new. The customer service representative must want to change and improve. That is essential, but it is not enough. That desire must be nurtured, rewarded and reinforced by management.

Over and over I have seen enthusiastic seminar attendees, eager to apply the tips and techniques they have picked up in class, return to a work environment where their best efforts are criticized or ignored. Many misguided supervisors are quick to jump on employees for any mistake while failing to notice all the times performance meets or exceeds expectations.

Sadly, in many companies, fear is still the motivator of choice. This is changing, but in my opinion, not fast enough. So what can be done? It's not that those in leadership positions don't want to do a good job. Many have simply never been educated about what it takes to motivate others to excellence.

Many years ago I made the transition from being an elementary-school counselor to being an in-service trainer in a 400-bed hospital. Not long after I arrived, the administrator over the entire nursing department asked for my help in dealing with a problem among the nursing staff. Morale was low and turnover was increasing. She was looking for ideas to help the management team better motivate the staff. Would I do a presentation for the nursing supervisors addressing those issues?

The very idea was intimidating. While I did have a master's degree in counseling, virtually all my professional experience at that time was with young children. What did I know about motivating adults?

Actually, I knew quite a lot. I just didn't realize it. My eight years of experience in trying everything I could to inspire students to learn had been an ideal training ground for understanding human needs, whether adult or child. In preparation for my presentation to the nurse supervisors, I decided to rely on common sense, the knowledge gained from my counseling education and the wisdom developed from working with hundreds of children. I entitled my talk, "Would A Kid Be Happy Here?" and I used five questions that children ask about any new environment they are about to enter, especially the common questions they ask when starting school.

The response was wonderful! I was relieved and delighted that what I shared seemed to really have an impact on the nurses. The woman who had made the original request was so pleased with the ideas I shared and the approach I had used that she asked me to speak to the entire administrative team. So, what concepts did we discuss? We addressed simple ideas for creating an environment where people can be their best — five small points that make a major difference in whether or not people succeed or merely survive.

Since that day I have studied and taught the newest and the best theories of management. I have been privileged to hear the highest-paid consultants and have spent time mastering some of the sophisticated language, techniques and measurement tools used in the complex world of leadership training. After all the education and exposure, I still believe that most of what I've learned can be summed up, clearly, simply with those same five points. Here are the five questions any supervisor, manager, or leader can ask to discover the answer to the question, *Would a Kid Be Happy Here?*

Is this a safe place? For most of us physical safety in the work place is not a major concern. Those work environments in which physical safety is a constant issue have taken great precautions to ensure that workers practice safe work habits. No, physical safety isn't the most frequent fear experienced by employees.

So, why is this the first question? It is first because the real issue is emotional safety. Is this a place free from embarrassment? Humiliation? Harassment? Children would ask: "Will the others call me names? Will I be punished for making a mistake. Will those in charge tell us what to expect or wait until we do something wrong and fuss at us? Do they want me to succeed, or are they secretly hoping I will fail so they can feel superior?"

I once had a manager I'll call Ms. C who had attained significant power within the organization. She was highly competent and had worked hard to move up the ladder at a time when women were at a great disadvantage. Unfortunately, she didn't often use her power to motivate or empower others. Anytime she took a disliking to someone, particularly another woman, we knew that person's days were numbered. Ms. C could easily undermine an employee's efforts and make his or her life generally miserable. I actually read a management article that referred to female executives like Ms. C as queen bees, for obvious reasons, if you remember from science class what a queen bee does to the other female bees in the hive.

People often give themselves away without realizing it. A coworker and I once listened in silent astonishment as Ms. C described in a nonchalant way how she had passed a summer afternoon eliminating the worms in her fruit trees. She had used kitchen shears to cut off the heads of the worms. When I expressed repulsion at her extermination method and asked why she didn't just use insecticide, she replied by saying that snapping off the heads one by one was much more satisfying. She actually said it was "fun" to find a branch laden with worms so that she could snip, snip, snip. For some reason, no one ever felt safe working for Ms. C.

The truth is protection from physical harm has become an issue these days. We expect so much from those in customer service roles, and sometimes we put these people at risk in an effort to satisfy a customer who is out of control.

There have always been difficult customers. Yet it wasn't until 1997 that I began to hear shocking stories from customer service representatives about death threats. In one instance,

customers with mobil phone repair problems were taking out
their frustrations by threatening to throw the phone at the face
of the company representative attempting to help them.
Another courageous service woman faced down a man with
her cool-headed courtesy when he placed a gun on the counter
while demanding his phone repairs be made immediately.
Television specials and newspaper articles have appeared
about the abuse of flight attendants; all of us who travel
frequently have observed irate customers become hostile and
irrational when their requests are denied.

Clearly, customers have grown much more abusive
verbally. Threats of bodily harm are more and more common.
The mental toll on those abused is impossible to measure.
What is management doing to protect those on the front-line?

Today, shocking as it may seem, homicide is the number
one cause of death in the workplace for women. It is the
number two cause of death for men, following accidents.
Some of these deaths are perpetrated by customers. The phrase
the customer is always right is naive. A company should never
value profitability over the safety of its employees. What
about your work world? Do people feel safe? Physically?
Mentally? Emotionally?

The second question children will ask is, **Will they like
me?** Approval, acceptance and friendship are important
human needs. Over the years, many organizations have tried to
force employees to separate their personal lives from their
workday. Management tends to fear feelings on the job. As
adults, sometimes we get so cynical that we reject the idea of
needing friends at work. Yet the fact remains that we spend
more time on the job than we do with our families. That is
more true today than ever. It is essential that our need for
approval and affection be at least partially satisfied between 9
and 5. We need parties, coffee breaks, conversation with

friends, laughter, silliness and fun. Work is stressful enough without the burden of trying to be serious all the time.

The worst case I have ever seen was a large force of telephone service representatives who were responsible for answering complex questions from the general public. I was asked to do customer service training with these folks, who handled over 200 calls per shift. I was appalled to learn about the working environment. The rules and demands on these people made their lives miserable. These were low-paying jobs, with no hope for promotion. That was just the beginning of their troubles. They had short, rigid break times, for which they clocked in and out, but the break room had no refreshments, no comfortable seats, nowhere to relax. The cafeteria was on the other side of the building, so even the lunch period was rushed and stressful. They were not allowed to talk to anyone at their desks — not even to ask for help if they needed assistance in order to serve the customer. Worst of all, the supervisor had nothing nice to say about anyone. According to her, the whole bunch were, lazy, complaining, stupid and hopeless.

On a happier note, my experience in working with companies that provide exceptional service show clearly that some organizations realize employees are people first. Everyone needs to feel acknowledged as an individual with a family, hobbies, dreams and personality traits that make them stand out.

In researching my stress-management seminars, I discovered that there was a growing collection of evidence that laughter is a significant stress reliever. The more stressful and serious the work, the greater the need for humor, relaxation and camaraderie. In the hospital where I once worked, a respected surgeon was known for bringing a radio into the operating room. He played music and cracked jokes during surgery. No one ever accused him of not taking his work seriously. Remember Hawkeye and the gang from *Mash*? Humor was the only thing that made life in a war zone bearable.

For children, being liked by their peers is incredibly important, but it's not enough. They also need to know that the teachers and principal, custodians and lunchroom help like them too. Adults have the same need to be known, noticed and accepted by corporate team-members, support staff, and executives. Kids aren't ashamed to admit it. They want to be popular. We could learn from them. It's good to feel wanted, needed, and missed. And it doesn't hurt to know the person filling out our report card thinks well of us.

The third question is simple: **Is this a nice place?** Is it pretty, colorful, bright and clean? What about supplies and equipment? Does it smell pleasant? Will it be too cold or too hot? What about the food? If the food is yuk, I won't like it here. Will I have my very own desk? Can I bring stuff to make it feel like home? I sure hope so. Please, is there privacy? A place I can go to be by myself for a minute or two? And locks on the bathroom door? Please! Sterile work stations may seem like a good idea. The truth is, sterile anything isn't natural. I go into many different work settings during the year. The atmosphere varies dramatically. It takes only a few minutes to discover if the people feel happy and at home there — to know if creativity is valued and individuality is respected.

Now, as we consider the fourth question, let's get serious: **How hard is the work?** Schoolwork may seem like play to adults long removed from the classroom, but for the students, coloring and counting is challenging work. Youngsters will ask other students two things about their assignments: "Is it too hard?" and "Is it too easy?"

The first question is not difficult to understand. If the work is excessive, too difficult or more complicated than the student is ready to handle, there will be a pervading fear of failure. You'll observe a lot of fight-or-flight symptoms and frustrated children will give up. So will frustrated adults. "Is it too easy?" At first glance, it appears that adults and children alike want easy work. That's a misconception. Easy work soon becomes boring and tedious. We wonder, *why don't they give me something important to do? Don't they trust me? They must think I'm stupid.* Ironically, both work that is too hard and work that is too easy result in the same negative consequence: low self-esteem and burnout.

It may take awhile to surface, but finally you'll hear this last question: **What will I get for doing the work?** M&M's won't motivate them for long. They need the P&P's: *Praise and power.* Frequent feedback is the most potent form of behavior modification. We are most likely to neglect giving feedback when performance is solid. I was always astonished when one of my best students would quietly inquire, "Ms. Kitching, am I going to pass?" It was a clear indication that my feedback wasn't often enough or specific enough.

If the boss, manager or role model neglects to praise the employee, the impact on customer satisfaction is immediate and dramatic. In the October 1997 issue of *Fortune* magazine, there was an article making exactly this point. Entitled, "Bringing Sears Into the New World," the author detailed how customer service was being improved by paying attention to the quality of the management.

The single, most powerful tool the manager has for motivating others is the use of praise. Finally, the employee needs to feel empowered to do his or her job. Having the resources needed to perform the tasks and the authority to make decisions enables the customer service provider to do what needs to be done to delight customers. With just a few changes, management can make a dramatic impact on the quality of customer service in their organization. It all starts with treating employees with dignity, consideration and respect.

Bio — Patty Kitching

Original, authentic and humorous, Patty Kitching has captivated and educated audiences from coast to coast. She combines solid academic credentials with a wealth of practical experience. In over 1600 presentations across thirty-eight states and four Canadian provinces, people have laughed and learned from this master speaker. In her role as a Career Consultant, Patty has provided guidance, encouragement, and loads of practical help to thousands of professionals facing job loss or career change. Her own versatile career history, a Masters in Counseling plus a painful personal experience with job loss, enables her to empathize with those in her audience experiencing the traumatic challenge of career upheaval. Patty has been a successful business owner and full time Professional Speaker. As founder of "Speaking For You," a consulting and training company, she provides her audiences with cutting edge information and career strategies essential for success and prosperity in the 21st century.

Contact Information:
Speaking For You
4457 East Jones Bridge Road
Norcross, GA 30092
Phone: (770) 840-0675
Toll Free: (800) 352-3886
Fax: (770) 263-7919

Resource Listing

Sam Bartlett Seminars

PO Box 1353 Galax, VA 24333
Toll Free: 1-800-513-5832
E-mail: Sam@sambartlett.com

Meg McLeroy Croot

Creative Recommendations, Inc.
1310 Land O' Lakes Drive
Roswell, GA 30075
Phone: 770-645-2862
Fax: 770-645-2869
E-mail: mcroot99@aol.com
Web site: www.creative-rec.com

Jerry Fritz

975 University Avenue, Madison, WI 53706-1323
Phone: (608) 262-7331
Toll Free: (800) 292-8964
E-Mail: JLF@mi.bus.wisc.edu or JLF@mi.bus.wisc.edu

Patty Kitching

Speaking For You
4457 East Jones Bridge Road
Norcross, GA 30092
Phone: (770) 840-0675
Toll Free: (800) 352-3886
Fax: (770) 263-7919

Mark Rosenberger
WOW! Performance Coaching, Inc.
10680 Loire Avenue, San Diego, CA. 92131
Phone: (619) 578-7900
Fax: (619) 578-7065
E-Mail: wowseminar@aol.com

Doug Smart, CSP
Doug Smart Seminars
P.O. Box 768024 Roswell, GA 30076
Phone: (770) 587-9784
Fax: (770) 587-1050
E-mail: DougSmart.Seminars@att.net

Jo Spurrier
Alliance, Inc.
417 NE 15th Avenue, Ft. Lauderdale, FL 33301
Phone: (954) 527-0140
E-mail: ALLIANCEjo@aol.com

Mike Stewart, CSP
Stewart & Stewart, Inc.
1140 Hammond Drive, Suite D4190, Atlanta, GA 30328
Phone: (770) 512-0022
Toll Free: (800) 422-5252
Fax: (770) 671-0023
E-mail: mstewart@mindspring.com

Liz Tahir
201 St. Charles Avenue
Suite 2500, New Orleans, LA 70170 USA
Phone: (504) 569-1670
Toll Free: (800) 506-1670
Fax (504) 524-7979
E-mail: liztahir@websiteventures.com

Index

Keeper Notes

Keeper Notes

Keeper Notes

Keeper Notes